Short Takes

Published by Merlyn's Pen, Inc.
4 King Street
P.O. Box 1058
East Greenwich, Rhode Island 02818-0964

Printed in the United States of America.

These are works of fiction. All characters and events portrayed in this book are fictional, and any resemblance to real people or incidents is purely coincidental.

Cover design by Alan Greco Design
Cover photography by John Van Beers
Section illustrations by Jane O'Conor
Artwork Copyright ©1994

Library of Congress Cataloging-in-Publication Data

Short takes : brief personal narratives and other works by American
    teen writers / edited by Kathryn Kulpa.
        p.   cm. -- (The American teen writer series)
    Originally published in Merlyn's pen.
    Summary: A collection of short fiction and personal narratives
written by students in grades six to twelve.
        ISBN 1-886427-00-3 : $9.75
        1. Short stories, American.   2. Youths' writings, American.
[1. Short stories.   2. Youths' writings.]   I. Kulpa, Kathryn.
II. Series.
PZ5. S565   1994
[Fic]--dc20   94-39802
                                                                    CIP
                                                                     AC

99 98 97 96 95   6 5 4 3 2

Short Takes

BRIEF PERSONAL NARRATIVES AND OTHER WORKS
BY AMERICAN TEEN WRITERS

Edited by
Kathryn Kulpa

The American Teen Writer Series
Editor: R. James Stahl

Merlyn's Pen, Inc.
East Greenwich, Rhode Island

Acknowledgments

The editor wishes to thank Joan Ayotte and Annette Schremmer for their editorial help as educational consultants.

All of the short stories in this book originally appeared in *Merlyn's Pen: The National Magazines of Student Writing*.

The American Teen Writer Series

Young adult literature. What does it mean to you?

Classic titles like *Lord of the Flies* or *Of Mice and Men*—books written by adults, for adult readers, that also are studied extensively in high schools?

Books written for teenagers by adult writers admired by teens—like Gary Paulsen, Norma Klein, Paul Zindel?

Shelves and shelves of popular paperbacks about perfect, untroubled, blemish-free kids?

Titles like *I Was a Teenage Vampire? Lunch Hour of the Living Dead?*

The term "young adult literature" is used to describe a range of exciting literature, but it has never accounted for the stories, poetry, and nonfiction actually written by young adults. African American literature is written by African Americans. Native American stories are penned by Native Americans. The Women's Literature aisle is stocked with books by women. Where are the young adult writers in young adult literature?

Teen authors tell their own stories in *Merlyn's Pen: The National Magazines of Student Writing*. Back in 1985 the magazine began giving young writers a place for their most compelling work. Seeds were planted. Ten years later, The American Teen Writer Series brings us the bountiful, rich fruit of their labors.

Older readers might be tempted to speak of these authors as potential writers, the great talents of tomorrow. We say: Don't. Their talent is alive and present. Their work is here and now.

Contents

Medium Shots

Wide Angles

The Reflecting Lens

Stories of identity and the self

A Toasted Night With a Cherry on Top

by Kerren Berger

I t was a common summer night. Humidity hung in every atom of the thick air. The only sound was heavy breathing from the bed next to me, occupied by my sister.

I couldn't go to sleep, partly because of my stifling cold and partly because of my anticipation of the next day. My mom had said that tomorrow was going to be a surprise. Where were we going that would take two hours to get to?

Sweat clung to my aching body and saturated my T-shirt. I finally mustered enough strength to sit up. I did this with such hardship that my feet fell asleep in the effort. I don't know what caused this.

I looked out my small window into the night. There was a big bright moon hanging bluntly in the sky, giving off a magic glow. I wondered if there really is a man in the moon.

My sister turned over as though she were as light as air. What right did she have not to sweat? Did she know about tomorrow? I couldn't stand the pressure anymore, so I did what I always do to relieve stress. I heave-hoed to the bathroom, picked up my toothbrush and toothpaste, and poured the red paste onto my special orthodontic toothbrush. Then I proceeded to brush my teeth as if there was no tomorrow. Back and forth, up and down. Afterwards, they were as white as ivory and as bright as a twinkling of dawn over fir trees. This sensation always cheered me up and cooled me down.

I stole downstairs to catch a glimpse of some movement, some life. Gladiator, my cat, who's probably heavier than I am, meowed his sad song, and it quite startled me. He was sitting on the old orange couch with his hind legs in the sleeping position, but his front legs alert and up. Gladiator's white face peered at me with a look as if to say, "I'm lonely, pet me. I need a good hug." Even the couch begged me to sit on it.

I consented. With a big plop, I settled myself willingly into years of the past. This couch represented my birth, my parents' marriage, and other little events.

As I stroked Gladiator, my heart started pounding. I spouted off about everything possible: What's life? Am I really alive? Are you listening to me? Each stroke had a different tone; each sang a different song.

I forgot all about the heat and the next day. The atmosphere was so full of silence and coziness that I sank into its arms and it caressed me. Drifting off to sleep, I felt a big cat in my arms and a chip off my shoulder.

Kerren Berger
Leawood Middle School, Leawood, Kansas

Through the Night Fog

by Barbara Jo Wrzos

S ilently, swiftly, I headed through the night fog. The dripping wet mass was so thick you couldn't see your own hand in front of your face. It felt like a hundred wet spider webs slapping against my body. I tried to whistle into the dark air, but even that seemed sad and forlorn. I paused and tried to figure out where I was. Let's see. It's four blocks from the sporting goods store and . . . What was that? Was that the sound of a single step in the gray mist, or was my mind playing tricks? I tried to concentrate on my bearings. Four blocks from the sporting goods store where I got my knife and . . . wait! There it was again! No, no, I must be mistaken. The only sound was the silence. "Stop being foolish!" I told myself. So I continued on toward my destination, though I couldn't shake the feeling I was being followed. My pulse quickened, my heart began to beat. Ahh, at last I came upon it— a lone streetlight that barely cast a glow on the darkened world. There I sat and waited. And waited. Finally I began to hear footsteps in the distance! As the brisk steps approached, my adrenaline began to pump and my heart beat so loudly I thought the whole world could hear it. Then, before I knew it, she was standing right in front of me, two grocery bags in her hands—easy prey. I was upon her in a flash. She didn't utter a sound. When the deed was done, I walked silently home.

Faint traces of fog lingered through the morning, but even if the world had finally come to its stormy end, I still would've felt marvelous. I reached outside to get the morning paper and looked at the headline. A feeling of competence swept over me as I read my favorite line: NIGHT STALKER STRIKES AGAIN: VICTIM #7.

Barbara Jo Wrzos
Fridley Middle School, Fridley, Minnesota

There's Nothing Like a Good Book

by Kate Stainer

I turn the pages of the book. My eyes focus on the black print. I slip further and further away from my own sense of reality with each word I read. Suddenly, I am swept along by the story like a leaf caught in the current of a river. I am swirled into dark and frightening whirlpools and tossed deeper and deeper until I am aware only of the scary silence of the black water.

My room—once spattered with clothing and scattered with papers and schoolbooks—is gone. The hand that waited to turn the next page is no longer a part of me. Are the cries of fear that I hear my own? Am I a brush stroke in this picture of horror?

Suddenly, I am catapulted toward the surface of the once dark, silent river, and without warning the screaming river smashes me up onto the shore. All is now quiet as I float back to the surface of reality. Once again I see my dirty jeans draped over the dresser and my battered chemistry book lying in the corner.

The sound of the river slapping against the shore has become footsteps echoing up the hall, and a voice outside my door says, "Kate?"

"Yes," I answer.
"Telephone!"

Kate Stainer
Oakland Mills High School, Columbia, Maryland

Another World

by Lee Farrell

My strange world used to worry me. Full of mystery, it made me feel like I was in constant danger. One of the things that used to frighten me most was the lack of space. All around me I saw large objects, but when I tried to venture closer, I was stopped by an invisible wall. There was a limit to how far I could travel. This always made me feel trapped.

Another thing that made me feel trapped was the feeling that I was being watched. I had good reason to believe that, and even now I still believe I'm being spied on once in a while.

Time of day was confusing at first. There was instant night, and there was instant day. Daylight would suddenly hit without warning and momentarily blind me. After a long day, the night would hit as quickly as day had come, plunging me into total darkness.

Daytime used to bring horror. I noticed blurs going by me, but they would be gone before I could tell what they were. The part that scared me was that sometimes the blurs would stay steady for a moment or two and I would notice an object, or creature of some sort, with what I guessed were eyes peering at me from the other side of the invisible wall. (This is how I got the feeling I was being watched.)

One strange thing I like about my world is that every day, weird, colorful flakes fall from the sky and drift by me. After some time, I experimented and found that the flakes tasted good and filled me up.

Lots of things confuse me in my world, but I am becoming used to ignoring them. I enjoy exploring the space that I do have, for it is filled with interesting things to see.

Well, darkness has just arrived. I guess I will swim behind my favorite rock again and sleep till morning. (*Glub! Glub! Glub!*)

Lee Farrell
Tri-City Jr. Academy, Pasco, Washington

No More "Dirty Look Special"

by Kathryn McKenzie

I t was a sunny spring morning. My mom was in the bathroom brushing her teeth, and I was impatiently waiting for her to finish. She put her toothbrush away and began walking out of the bathroom. "Wait!" I called excitedly. As I stood beside her, peering into the mirror, I noticed something very strange. Something was very different.

"Finally!" I cheered. "It's about time!" We looked closer, just to make sure that it was true.

She looked at me sadly. "I guess this means a lot to you."

I asked my dad and my sister to verify it for me. Yup, it was true. I was finally taller than my mother!

For most of you, this is really no big deal; for me, however, it is very exciting. Being tall is a great asset in the sports world. It allows you to look down on everyone and feel important. I checked every couple of days to see if I had finally surpassed her in growth. Passing the microwave or patio doors, I would sneak a peek at our reflections to see if the moment had arrived. So today was a glorious day! I could now float above the world and feel important like she did. And now I would feel even more important, for I was taller than my mother!

My mom is a woman of above-average height. She carries herself with dignity and pride. Towering at 5′8″, she uses her height to intimidate the young children who walk the hallways at the school where she works. She's also used it to her advantage when disciplining my sister and me. "Go to your room!" A loud voice would descend from on high, intensifying the scoldings. When she spoke, I listened. When she looked down upon me while giving her "Dirty Look Special" (the deadly glare), I felt helpless and inferior. As I matured and demanded certain privileges, she would simply stare me down, saying that I was not yet old enough. Deep down inside, I knew that it was mainly because I couldn't meet her eye to eye.

Through constant arguments at the beginning of my teenage years, she would give me her overpowering look, stand up tall, and tell me point-blank that I was wrong. "When you're a mother, you'll understand." But of course I was always right because, after all, I was a teenager. Again, she just would not listen to the opinions of a person at whom she had to lower her eyes to communicate. Yes, to get respect, I would have to grow—not become a mother.

So finally, that day, I had broken the curse! No more scoldings, no more wrong opinions, and no more "Dirty Look Specials." Now I was the one giving the withering looks.

I'm not sure exactly why, but giving the "Dirty Look Special" no longer satisfies me. Maybe it's because my eyes get sore from prolonged glaring, or maybe it's because I don't feel quite so important anymore. One thing I do know is that things have changed.

My mother and I don't really argue anymore. We talk and discuss things like civilized people. We share stories and tell jokes. We think about the good things that have happened, and the good things that are about to come.

Maybe it's because I've grown in more important ways.

Kathryn McKenzie
College Jeanne-Sauvé, Winnipeg, Manitoba, Canada

Through My Picture Window

by Ami Palmer

My spacious backyard lies spread out before me like a gypsy's shawl. I hear the faint chirping of robins, and occasionally one swoops down from a tree and glides to the other side of the yard. From time to time, the wind picks up fallen brown leaves and carries them swirling away to one of the overgrown flower beds. A lone tomcat slinks craftily along the fence, his gray-striped belly brushing bare patches of earth. A peeling picnic table sits crookedly in a large circle of dirt where a swimming pool used to be. Beyond the ancient table lies a sagging clothesline, which a yellow delicious apple tree embraces with its twisted branches. Rotten apples clutter the base of the tree like Christmas gifts. A Styrofoam archery target is leaning crazily against a shed, waiting for a strong gust to send it careening across the yard.

To the right of the yard, beneath the shadows of several tall locust trees, rest the remains of four deceased pets: a cat, a dog, and two hamsters. Only two grave markers guard the burial ground, as the hamsters are entombed with the dog and cat. A sandbox rests, overflowing, to one side of the graves. In it, my brother has built the beginning of a clubhouse from old, gray boards and the frame of a rusty swing set. Tall climbing rosebushes reach toward the top of the fence, their buds glistening with fat, green aphids. A blue wheelbarrow tilts upright under the rickety redwood deck like a tin soldier guarding a palace.

To the left, a black iron rail borders cement stairs that lead downstairs to the back door. An old, chocolate-colored freezer with a rope tied around its door stands dejectedly behind the stairs. Directly above it is a metal pole that we use to hang up the hummingbird feeder in warmer weather. It stands bare now, except for a pine cone that has been tied on with a pipe cleaner. Long ago the pine cone was a bird feeder that I made in kindergarten. In the back corner of the yard rests a tin shed in which we keep our garden tiller. Its faded, green sides reflect the sun savagely. Beside the shed is a pitch-covered swing set, or what's left of it. All that remains now is a broken seat and chains. The wind blows harder, and I hear the slight tinkling of rusty wind chimes. Sensing rain, I close the window and click on the television.

Ami Palmer
West Jr. High School, Boise, Idaho

Always a Memory

by Thomasine Peltier

Alone at home, I stare into the dormant fireplace. A charred piece of wood lies among the ashes. That area of the room is darkened, the bricks dull around the fireplace. Everything mirrors my cold emptiness.

This feeling comes and goes, a feeling that I've lost something valuable. Always it's a memory of something I've lost—friends, an old school, my bird Sweetie. Sweetie's death didn't touch me at first, but as time passed, her absence would bring on nightmares. I'd cry out her name so that I could feel I was not alone. There would be no answer. I'd call out again, and I still wouldn't get that familiar yawn or movement within her cage. I'd get nothing but silence.

Still staring into the fireplace, I get up and flick on the light. Even though the living room is now lit up, my empty feeling doesn't go away. I still feel like I've lost something close to me—my friends, a school I used to attend and love, my bird, and the person I used to be: that little girl, immune to loss.

Thomasine Peltier
Traverse City Jr. High School, Traverse City, Michigan

Red Skies

by Alice Reagan

I work in a bakery on Saturdays. It's a decent job, I guess. I love how the bread smells, fresh and warm out of the oven. I have to wear a blue uniform, and I always manage to get flour all over it by the end of my shift. Most of the people who come in are nice, unassuming types. Occasionally, though, we get your garden-variety weirdo. Take last Saturday, for instance.

It was almost 3:30 and I was just cleaning up around the store—wiping the counters, spraying the glass cases—when this man came into the empty store. He wasn't very tall, and he had dark hair and a thick Greek accent when he opened his mouth to order a birthday cake for the following week. I took the order, asking what color frosting and what name to write on top.

When I was finished, he leaned his forearm, which was very hairy, across the counter and bent his face right next to mine—so close that if I just inched forward our noses would touch. I didn't know quite what to do, so I didn't do anything. He lowered his eyes to about my midsection, opened his mouth and asked me, all bedroom eyes and Greek accent and about 45 years old: "Are you in love?"

I remember thinking, *Uh-oh,* and then, for lack of something clever to say, just smiling at him, and then kind of spacing out and forgetting he was there. I saw myself on a winter night two months ago with Paul. He and I decided to go ice-skating at the lake near his house. We walked down without talking, our skates tied over our shoulders and bouncing slightly against our backs, holding hands through our gloves. We skated and laughed and fell down on the hard, snowy ice for a while, the sky a strange red color over our heads, the air cold and at the same time not cold, until we got tired. Then we danced together, holding each other with our whole bodies touching through layers of sweaters and jackets, our breath coming warm out of our mouths. I thought I loved him. The thought was so sweet, so real in my mind, that I could hardly bear it.

Then I flashed to a scene from less than a week ago—me sitting on my bed, curled up in a little ball, talking to my best friend Terry, telling her about how Paul had dumped me for Karen O'Shea, a cheerleader. It was stupid to cry so much, I realized later. Paul was very nice about the whole thing, but at the time I felt angry and hurt.

I must have been daydreaming for only a second, because when I came back, the man was still looking at me expectantly, waiting for an answer.

"No, not today," I said.

I knew right away that it was a good answer, one that he hadn't heard before, because he smiled his alligator-tooth smile at me and had to think for a moment.

"Maybe tomorrow you will be in love?" he teased.

Slight pause. "Maybe."

The man smiled again, searching my face, having met his match. When I turned away to continue cleaning, he finally left. I thought about him for a while, and then I thought about his silly question. I don't know what made me say 'maybe,' but it sure seemed right. The world is full of wonderful possibilities, even for a temporarily boyfriendless, non-cheerleader like me.

Alice Reagan
Bishop Fenwick High School, Peabody, Massachusetts

Without the Imagination

by Henry Clarke

Orphaned at birth, I'd grown up in the Missoula Home for Boys. I was born there, but never left with my mother. I doubt she ever saw me. I was never breast-fed; they say I accepted a bottle on the first try. I didn't even have the instincts of a regular boy.

We were not allowed to watch television at the Home (*Home* always emphasized by the attendants), and I'm glad. The typical television family might have overwhelmed me. I couldn't have watched Dennis Mitchell play with Mr. Wilson in suburbia while I sat unwanted, wedged in the armpit of Montana.

So my years at the Home were spent squirming in school (I completed grade twelve) and tending the small animals kept out behind the central building. I loved the dogs and goats and sheep that lolled in the back. The parents of the newborns would protect them from the wild animals and from foul weather, and once I became familiar to the animals, they would protect me also. After dark, I'd sit on the ground, patting the dogs, and they would gather around and lie near me. Once, when we heard a coyote, they all got up and circled me, their hackles raised in my defense.

When I finally left the Home at eighteen (I was the oldest resident in the Home's history), they gave me Lady, my favorite black Lab. I'd trained her from birth when I was thirteen; she was my best friend. The people at the Home said she had very fancy parents, but the owners couldn't cope with all the puppies, so they gave one to the Home. When they gave me her pedigree (not the kind of thing often found at an orphanage), I read her full name: Repentant Lady. I threw out the slip of paper and renamed her Mary.

I drove through Montana, making money wherever I could. I cut grass in Brockway, scrubbed dishes in Vandalia, and sold TVs at a Radio Shack in Polson on the edge of Flathead Lake. As I drove from job to job, Mary would lie quietly on the seat of my truck, and I'd rub her soft ears as I drove. My independence made me feel adult and mature. It also made me think of what it would be like to have a family, of how wonderful it would be to be driving home for Christmas.

Sometimes I'd see myself in the mirrors as I looked around at Montana, and I'd fantasize about what my mother looked like. I was sure she was pretty, but not beautiful. I didn't have the dainty features that a beautiful mother dictates in her offspring. She was probably of average height, since I was just under six feet. I also knew she would be young, because orphans are usually left by young mothers. I'd look at every woman I saw and compare them to myself, hoping someday to find a match.

I liked to think of my mother as a glamorous woman, but I did not see her in Great Falls or at a ski resort. I thought I saw her once, in a town later identified to me as "the one between Cohagen and Jordan." I had a road atlas, but there was no marked town along that stretch of Montana.

The ability of the human to live on hope is incredible. Long, cold, rainy nights were made palatable by the thought of my mother. As a grade-school student can get through math class by thinking about stickball at recess, so could I get through huge spells of loneliness by imagining my mother; she, too, must have been searching.

Mary was sitting on the seat beside me when I pulled in to the small diner along the side of Route 59. She was pregnant, due any day. I'd bred her to a stud in Great Falls; I needed the money her pups would bring. I'd never had a family, so I wondered what I'd do when Mary's family appeared. Her stomach bulged under her, seeming to sweep the ground, and, when she ran, her overflowing teats flapped and slapped against each other like a screen door against its frame. In the latter part of her pregnancy, Mary had become very protective of me; she wouldn't let strangers advance on me without barking and raising the fur on the back of her neck. She worried, too. She'd walk tiny circles on the seat of the truck, sniffing and exploring the same two feet of synthetic leather again and again; then she'd flop wearily down in the middle of her circle. I would just look over at her and wait for the puppies to arrive, right there in the Ford. She would lie very close to me and put her head in my lap.

The diner was disheveled. An overflowing dumpster squatted off to one side, and a decrepit row of cabins stood behind the restaurant. The curtains were orange and brown, dusty and ripped, and the coverings on the booths and counter stools inside were vinyl; bits of stuffing jutted out from the seats.

I usually looked for my mother in public places—movie theaters or restaurants. Some people showed traits that I exhibited, the same jawbone, the same rhythm of breathing, but never more than one or two parts of me would match anyone else. I knew that someday I'd find my mother, and she would just know me and we'd love each other and take care of each other.

I entered the diner through the ripped screen door, sat down at the counter, and ordered a cup of coffee and a huckleberry muffin. The lady running the place was grotesque: huge bags hanging below her eyes, and girdled blobs of fat pushing out around her cinched apron. Canadian bacon popped on the long griddle behind her, coating the splatter-guard with grease and warm fat. A 45 spun in an old juke-box that was pushed back into the corner, its lights flickering as the bulbs wore down. The coffee was good, but the muffin was stale. It was dried out, and the berries were dispersed in a thoughtless pattern. I filled Mary's water dish from a sink in the grungy little bathroom of the diner and plodded out to the dirt parking area in front.

As I settled the water container in the dust, a little red jeep swerved into the lot, throwing dust over its outside wheels. A tall woman stepped out, her cowboy boots settling in the dirt. She was in fashionable dress: her gripping jeans tucked into the boots, and a denim shirt tied at the bottom, exposing her navel. Her flat chest and straight hips were hardly feminine, but her face was attractive, blue eyes like my own dominating her other features. I guessed she was about thirty-five. She looked more wealthy than anyone else in that part of Montana. The jeep was clean and in good condition. She dressed in the current style.

I followed her back into the diner. Her features were similar to my own, and I imagined that her picture in my fictional living room would not look out of place.

She sat at the counter but ordered nothing. The fat woman passed her a 'good morning' and set a cup of black coffee beside her. Her hips expanded over the small round stool as she rolled to one side to reach the cup. She picked her boots up from the footrest under the counter and crossed her legs. She sat elegantly, but her dusty face defeated her clothes in their attempt at an image that was greater than she could support. She wasn't royalty, but she held herself as if she were. Her chin paralleled the counter, pointing her eyes at the wall over the skillet. Her ears twitched a little when she blinked.

Her body fit the picture of my mother that I had constructed over my lifetime. Her features were very similar to mine, and any father could make up for the differences. I stared at her for a long time. She sat as I did, and when she spoke to the cook, her sweet voice had the same tone as mine.

She could have raised me in a little ranch house, riding horses and living together for years. She could

have loved me all my life, never regretting her decision to keep me. Instead, I had been discarded at
birth. But that could be forgiven. I could forget all
that and take her now with any past we chose. She
was a perfect match. All her features matched my
own—her hair, her cheeks, her eyes.

It is amazing that I was still letting my mind race
into fantasies of a family and of a mother. After almost twenty years of being an orphan, I should have
hardened myself against the hope of ever finding
her. I knew she would never simply announce herself at the Missoula Home for Boys and whisk me
away. I knew as well as I knew my times tables that
she would not drive up and take me to a farm and
raise me in the Corn Belt. But a human body does
not allow its user to abandon hope. Hope fuels the
body, a hope that better times and a better life are
on the way, maybe just a day away.

I knew this woman was my mother after a few
moments of studying her, but then she did something that convinced me so much I was ready to in-
troduce myself.

My mother looked deliberately at me and said,
flat in tone, with no emotion, "It's so nice that the
sun's out today."

I said nothing. I could say nothing. She knew I
was her son. I had found my mother after agonizing
years of hope and grievance. She wanted me back.
She hadn't wanted to give me up—she'd been forced
to—and wonderful fate had brought us to the same
point on this day of our separate quests.

A Volkswagen sputtered into the lot, and my
mother looked away from me and stood up stiffly.

She walked past me to the door. She greeted the man who got out of the car with a kiss on the cheek. He was disgusting; his skin was pale and rutty, and his business suit was grimy and of an unpleasant cut. He was very thin, and his thick beard made his head appear too heavy for the rest of him. His inflated head made me wonder if he ever had to prop it up to keep it from tumbling off and rolling down his horrid suit.

The two walked to one of the dilapidated cabins behind the diner and quickly went in. I followed and stopped just around the corner. They drew the blinds hurriedly and locked the door. I watched intently for half an hour, then saw them come back out. The man had forgotten to put his tie back on, and the woman's hair hung down out of its style. Her shirt was untied, and not buttoned far enough up to hide her tiny breasts. He gave her a wad of bills and walked to the front of the diner. He opened the door to his shabby compact and plopped in. The car popped away down Route 59.

She entered the back of the diner through a small plywood door and tiny hall that led her behind the counter. I looked into the building through the ripped curtains and saw my mother give some of the bills to the old woman behind the counter. They laughed as my mother tied her hair back out of her face.

I stared at the small cabin where my mother had offended me so many times. I was starting for the truck when I heard Mary yelp from somewhere in the bushes. She had been loose in the lot since my mother drove up, and had wandered off behind the dumpster. I called to her, but she only barked back from the same place. I crashed into the bushes and found her beneath a berry bush, kindly licking clean her pups. There were four, all black. Their fur was slicked back like a teenager's in the Fifties, their eyes closed like frightened children's in a spookhouse. Mary stood up to greet me and revealed one dead pup, crushed by the weight of its mother.

I gathered up the living puppies and put the dead one in the dumpster. I thought that Mary might get upset, so I let her watch me, but she didn't care about the dead one; it was no longer her responsibility. I put them in my coat on the seat of the truck. Mary waddled into the truck, the pain and effort of delivery still with her. She licked them all again, and then allowed them to feed from her abundant supply of breast milk.

Pulling out of the diner, I let my mind go black. I stared at the white line on the side of the road, not seeing anything of Montana as it rushed by me. I put a horse blanket over Mary and her pups and tried desperately to keep them within its warmth, but they always squirmed their way out.

Every time I saw myself in the mirror I became enraged. I'd pound on the wheel of the truck, scaring Mary and her puppies. Sometimes I would thrash myself into tears, then collapse, drooping over the wheel and cursing my taunting reflection as it looked at me from the windshield. I could see my mother everywhere.

I ran deeper into the state, my eyes fixed on the broken white line, my gas gauge slowly winding down. I ran out of gas climbing a huge deserted mountain, my foot heavy on the accelerator. I gripped the wheel of the truck for a long time, just staring at the white line and concentrating on the road ahead of me. Hoping that the truck would have a sudden surge of power and travel on its own, or that I would be rescued . . .

As the sun began its descent behind the mountain, I eased out of my position in the cockpit and put my back against the seat. My fingers were cramped from hours of strangling the steering wheel, and my right leg was tingly numb. Lying down on the seat, I put my head on the edge of the blanket, curled up against Mary and her sleeping babies, and sobbed.

Henry Clarke
Phillips Exeter Academy, Exeter, New Hampshire

Close-Ups

Stories of family, friendship, and relationships

Ernie

by Jeff Pride

When Ernie was about one year old, we brought him on vacation with us. This turned out to be an experience none of us would ever forget.

The plans were made and we were ready to go. After we hitched the boat and trailer to the car, my dad gave everything one last safety check. We were renting a camp on an island, on Lake Wentworth in New Hampshire, about a three-and-a-half-hour drive from Coventry, where we live.

After about an hour, Ernie became carsick. My dad had to find a place to pull over on the highway and let him out. After we finished cleaning up the car and Ernie had some fresh air, we were ready to roll again. This time my dad tied Ernie to a leash in the boat hitched to our car. This way, he could get fresh air and move around a little, without being able to jump out.

We started down the highway again, and my dad, who likes to make good time on a trip, remarked that we were already one hour behind schedule. Cars were whizzing by us and people were smiling and laughing and pointing in our direction. At first we didn't know why we were getting all this attention. Then we looked back, and there was Ernie sitting up behind the steering wheel of the boat. His long beagle ears were flying in the wind and his paws were on the wheel as if he were racing everyone who passed by.

Jeff Pride
Coventry Jr. High School, Coventry, Rhode Island

Grandpa's Hand

by Juli Peterson

I was only about four when he held his hand out to me. I took it in mine and we walked. Then I asked him, "Grandpa, why do you have so many wrinkles on your hand?"

He laughed and said, "Well, Grandson, that's a grand question!" He was silent for a moment. He must have been thinking.

This was his answer: "Each one of these wrinkles stands for a trouble I've had through my years, and each of the troubles I've lived through."

I looked at his other hand. "But Grandpa," I said. "How come you have even more on that one?"

"Those are for all the glories and joys in my life."

"Grandpa," I said. "May I count them?"

Juli Peterson
Libby Middle School, Spokane, Washington

Remember

by Kevin Kitching

I n every person's life there is one person who can change everything. This person rarely stays very long, just long enough . . .

Her name was Chris. I don't know her last name, and I don't think I want to. If I did, I would probably spend a long time trying to find her.

I was not a lover to her. In fact, we had not known each other long enough to become friends. But after one night on a Greyhound bus, I knew her very well.

We had spent the better part of that night talking about ourselves. We talked about our different problems, how they affected us, and, most importantly, why they affected us. I learned that you can uncover a lot about a person just by finding out why certain things bother them. And after she fell asleep in my arms, I looked at my watch and saw that we had talked the night away.

Things started flowing through my mind. Would I ever see her again? God, I wanted to. With every fiber in my body, I wanted to.

Later, the sunlight filtered through the pre-dawn

haze, throwing a sunbeam on Chris's face. She opened her eyes and without squinting looked into mine. Then she closed her eyes and fell back to sleep. Only seconds later, I fell into a deep, contented sleep.

It was midafternoon when I awoke. Something was wrong. I opened my eyes and saw that she was gone. In her seat was a scrap of paper. The note read, SORRY I DID NOT WAKE YOU, BUT YOU WERE SLEEPING TOO SOUNDLY. THANK YOU FOR THE ARMS, THE SHOULDER, AND ESPE-CIALLY FOR THE UNDERSTANDING. I WILL HOLD A PLACE IN MY HEART FOR YOU. LOVE, CHRIS.

I stared off into the forests of Alabama and cried in the distant reaches of my mind.

I still have the note somewhere. I may throw it away the next time I come upon it. I don't know, maybe I'll keep it just to keep it. Just another piece of junk in a dusty corner of my desk. That's all I need—more junk. If I throw it away, I will still re-member, and that's enough for me.

Kevin Kitching
Garfield Independent Learning Center, San Diego, California

Heat Wave

by Kelcey Terrell

It was hot. We couldn't decide whether to leave the windows up and turn the air conditioning on, or roll the windows down and hope we would soon drive through a pocket of cool air to relieve our sweaty faces. The air in the car was like a sauna, singeing the hair in my nose as I inhaled. The ice cubes left over from my Coke that we had bought at Dairy Queen melted in about two seconds, turning into lukewarm, Coke-flavored water. Heat waves shimmered on the highway ahead, making it look like a lake had covered the asphalt. But as we came closer, it would disappear and move farther down the road. The car gave a gasp, and my dad looked at the instrument panel. The indicator was creeping into the red section on the temperature gauge. My dad swore under his breath and pulled over. As he took the cap off the radiator, a spout of steam rose and burned his hand. I sighed and wiped the trickle of sweat that was sliding down the tip of my nose and dreamed of snowmen and icicles.

Kelcey Terrell
Joel E. Ferris School, Spokane, Washington

Mike's Room

by J.M. Matteson

I hope all the junk in this room crawls up on your bed and tears the flesh from your bones."

"Really, Mom, that's disgusting."

"I'm sick of this mess greeting me all the time at the door."

"Then stop coming in."

"Wait till your father gets home."

"Ooo, then he can come on in an' join the fun," Mike finished tiredly.

Thankfully (and with obvious exaggeration), Mom slammed the door. Mike was getting tired of her sermons. "More hellfire than a Southern preacher on Sunday," as Dad would say. It was his room; why should she care what it looked like? It wasn't her duty in life to live in it, look at it, sing to it, or pick it up. Oh yeah—the Levi shrink-to-fits were going to climb over the edge of the bed and suck his brains out. Or, better yet, his socks might. She reminded him of something. Rice Krispies. All they did was make noise.

Mike threw his fifteen-year-old body down on his lovely blue sailboat sheets, causing the bedsprings to cry out in agony. Shaking all thoughts of carnivorous rooms, as well as the highly ridiculous picture of Mom singing "Twist and Shout" to the mass of clutter strewn strategically about the floor, he drifted into a half-sleep.

His daze was broken by a nudge against his neck. The nudge turned to a burn as a sweat sock wound itself around Mike's throat. A striped oxford shirt then secured his waist, and before he could budge, two economy-sized packages of Fruit of the Loom pinned down his arms and legs. Heaps of papers, clothing, fermented sandwiches, an acoustic guitar, a couple of plates, and a girlie magazine of Dad's that Mike had stashed under his bed (January issue, 1982) dragged themselves from the floor, closet, and dresser (which sat at an odd angle with its drawers ejected at different levels) to create an ornate and colorful tomb. . . .

Mom stood at the top of the stairs, preparing to deliver one of her most impassioned speeches. Reaching a feverish pitch, she let her hands fly into the door, crashing it open.

Viewing the scene, she almost collapsed in shock. Every single piece of Mike's refuse had been put away. But something else captured her attention, too. In the exact center of the bed was a neat, orderly and quite proper pile of bones.

J.M. Matteson
New Berlin Central School, New Berlin, New York

Have I Told You Lately?

by Aaron Skolnik

Notes from the piano filled the room as if riding on the tiny particles of light skimming the pale walls. The small, candlelit tables were empty. A solitary light bulb behind the bar made the whole diner seem as if from a black and white movie. The full October moon shone brightly through the window like a warm spotlight on the dusty gray tones of the tile floor.

He held her in his arms tightly, drawing in the soft scent of her Youth Dew perfume. Her hands moved slowly up and down his back as she closed her eyes and lay her blond head across his broad shoulder. Van Morrison's low, raspy voice echoed softly, and the record spun slowly on the turntable in the corner. "Fill my heart with gladness, take away my sadness, ease my troubles—that's what you do . . ." Joe slid his arms around her waist and led her in a slow circle, making rings in the thin layer of dust on the well-scuffed dance floor. He kissed her neck gently, and she whispered, "I love you, Joe." He answered without a second thought, "I love you too." The lines of the moonlit area became less distinct as the whole diner faded away.

His unmoving eyes focused on the vivid techni-
color room around him, and voices interrupted his
favorite song. "Everything is in order, Mrs. Harper,"
came a low, masculine voice. "I'll leave you two
alone for a moment to say goodbye."

"Thank you, doctor," came the reply. A familiar
face blocked out the bright fluorescent light above
him. Her hair, though no longer blond, still shone
with a radiance Joe had never seen in another. "Joe,"
she whispered, "I know you probably can't hear me
or understand me, but I just want you to know that I
still love you just as much as I ever did. I always will.
Goodbye, Joe . . ." He felt her kiss on his forehead,
and the song drifted back in . . .

"Have I told you lately that I love you? Have I
told you there's no one above you? . . ." There was
more muffled speech in the background, and, as
Joe's heels cut crescents in the dust on the floor, he
felt a tube being pulled from his mouth. He heard a
hum, the turntable's diamond needle slid from the
record's last groove with a soft *pop!*, and the diner
was no more.

Aaron Skolnik
Thomas Jefferson High School for Science and Technology,
Alexandria, Virginia

Addicted

by Una Kim

The girl inhaled the smoky aftermath, scowling at the source. The cigarette, barely held by his thin lips, hung low.

"I hate it when you smoke," she said. "You'll die an early death because of it."

The young man shrugged, his loose shirt hanging off his frame like rolls of skin on a decrepit grandfather. The dust, colored by the hidden Indian clay, rose in tiny clouds from the weathered road as he kicked the ground with the toe of his boot. He paused.

"I'll die when I'm good and ready," he said. Looking up, he focused on the approaching future until it stopped in front of him.

Swiftly, he reached up to his mouth, gently pulling the cigarette from his lips. Dropping his hand, he let go of the burning butt that had balanced so precariously between his slim, jaundiced fingers. With a heel, he crushed it into the dirt, leaving only a charred memory.

He began to board the third-rate bus when she reached to stop him.

"Call me when you get there?" she asked.

"Get where?" he answered.

She paused.

"Call me when you stop then," she recovered.

He nodded, shrugging her hand off his shoulder. He boarded the bus and she watched it disappear.

Slowly, she began shuffling home, kicking aimlessly at the grass lipping the road. The wind lapped her face rhythmically as she took a smokeless breath. She stared at the road ahead, cigarette butts scattered across the loose gravel, and ground them in with sagging steps.

Una Kim
Dulaney High School, Timonium, Maryland

Early Risers

by Marianne Smith

I leap down the creaky, chilly stairs, trying to keep up with my nose. The aroma of fresh bread floats up to make sure that I'm awake.

I lift the blue and white cloth that covers the bread and slice a piece. I slather on butter and homemade strawberry jam. The butter melts instantly. The bread is just hours old. I perch at the window and peer out to find the creator of the mouth-watering bread—Grandpa.

Even before the chickens wake up, Grandpa starts another day of hard work in the fields. The sun is just peeking over the cornstalks. He bends down and throws the weeds over his shoulder. Farmers call this "walking the beans." Grandpa, with 77 years gone by, still is doing the job of a lad.

I run upstairs and jump into my blue jeans, stiff from last week's ground-in dirt. I put on the shirt that Mom says makes me look like a ragamuffin, but do I care? NO!

I don't care whom I wake up, even though it is still only 6:30 A.M. The day is flying, and I'm not go-

ing to waste one more minute of it. I dance out to
help Grandpa.

Marianne Smith
Oyster River Middle School, Durham, New Hampshire

Blank Disks

by Morgan Heintz

I remember back to two years ago . . . He sat there in the wooden chair, bonded to the Macintosh by the white glare of the screen reflected onto his face. His fingers furiously typed, then slowed down. He thought, biting his upper lip, closing his eyes, with his head tilted back. And then . . . Wham! His eyelids sprinted back, revealing life, exhilaration. He typed again, now more wildly, rushing, making sure that he got all his ideas on the screen before he forgot them.

I remember back to two years ago . . . The sound of the ImageWriter creeping through my door—*connnndggo-in-do-ee!*—as I tried to sleep. I see the carriage sliding across the paper, leaving tracks of words from my brother's English report, then sliding back to the left and beginning again.

I remember back to two years ago . . . Walking into the small room with the windows on three of the four sides. The sun leaked through mini-blinds, bringing life and energy into the room. I brought my brother Nestlé chocolate chip cookies, warm from the first batch that I had just baked from scratch—a studying high-school student's vital survival food.

But that was when he was a part of Ms. Busy's English class.

My brother is leaving now. Accepted at Trinity College.

"Everything is packed," he says. When he says everything, he means tapes, posters, compact disks, stereo system, and some cologne to attract the girls.

We sent him his forgotten toothbrush.

Dad drove, Mom tried to tell old stories: "Remember the time you cut your hair and said that you were going to fire your old barber? . . ." Grover tried to sleep but I poked him, tickled him—anything to stop him from going to sleep and leaving me and his old life at home before we had to say good-bye. And even after that, I chased him to the dorm.

We went home. I cried while my parents thought I was sleeping under my jacket.

My brother is gone now. Off to college. He's taken the computer to his dorm room. I don't hear him typing anymore. He has graduated from his senior European History class—no more midnight essays to write.

My brother is gone now. Off to college. He has taken the ImageWriter, too. Falling asleep should be easy now. I have nothing to distract me but fond memories. And wishes.

My brother is gone now. Off to college. He's taken himself. Away. As I walk into the computer room, it's no longer a place I go to laugh. No glow fills the air, no cookie crumbs on the floor for Mom to yell about, no Grover. I have tried to fix it up. I have painted it, got a new floor, hung a picture of a beach scene, bought an upholstered chair, and even put in a bookshelf with colorful books that I don't read. Nothing can make it as special as it used to be.

My brother is gone now. Off to college. Cookies aren't very fun to bake when you have only yourself to share them with. Grover's not there anymore. No friendly person with eyes full of thanks, no brother smiling and telling me he'll do anything that I want for the rest of my life and that I'll always be his life-saver.

Morgan Heintz
Weston Middle School, Weston, Massachusetts

A List of 10 Things

by Loubel Cruz

There is a window right next to my seat in sixth-period literature that offers a view of the court-yard. Good thing, that window, for if it wasn't there, I would be asleep. I listened restlessly to Sister Mary Catherine lecture on and on about who the main characters were in *A Tale of Two Cities.* I watched the snow gently falling on the statue of St. Francis of Assisi, the patron saint after whom my school was named, amazed at how much snow had already accumulated. It was the beginning of February, and, being a native Texan, I was not used to foot-deep snow packs on my sidewalk every morning. But that's what you get when you move to Boston—home of the Red Sox, commercial fishing, and blizzards. I smiled at that thought, for it was exactly what Davis warned me about before I moved here, except he probably didn't know how right he was. I laughed inside when I thought of Davis. Then my heart began to hurt when I thought about how the move here was the most difficult thing I'd ever done. It all started above five months ago. Five months ago when the biggest event in my short, but unpredictable, fifteen years began.

It was a hot, humid day in October. The kind of day you wish the air conditioner was going full blast and that there was more ice in your lemonade and that you'd put on more deodorant that morning. I was living in Houston, Texas, where I'd lived all my life, and attended Duke Senior High, where I was a freshman.

"My parents are acting weird, all secretive and stuff," I told Davis Vaughn. It was worrying me, it really was.

We were sitting in my room after school and Davis was checking, or should I say copying, my geometry answers. He didn't like math, and never really tried at it. His favorite subject was gym. Davis was convinced he was going to become all-pro in every sport that ever existed and become a "kabillionaire." And even though he taunted me about my dream, which was to become a writer, I never once thought of shattering his hopes.

"Look, Marshall, everything will be OK. Your parents have just been hanging around mine too much. It makes them wacko too," Davis said, not taking his eyes off the postulates and theorems.

A couple of years ago he came up with this wonderful idea to call me by my last name—which is Marshall—instead of my first—which is Colleen. He said Colleen was too feminine. I said I was a girl. He said he wasn't sure. I said for him to stuff it. It was all annoying at first, but I got used to it.

Davis Vaughn is my best friend. I never really told him that, and now that I think of it, I never admitted it to anyone else; I bet he never has either. But we knew. We knew deep down and our friendship was so strong we didn't have to say it.

"Well, I'd better be going home now," Davis said, closing the geometry book. "It's broccoli quiche night. Don't worry, Marshall, everything will be cool."

I looked at him, storm clouds in my eyes.

"I promise." He smiled at me, his eyes sparkling. The "Davis sparkle," as I called it.

That night at dinner, I played with my food, occasionally forcing a small piece of lasagna down my throat. My parents kept looking at me funny, very curious about what my problem was. Good, that's what I wanted; I wanted to know what was wrong, too.

"Colleen, sweetie, is anything wrong?" my mom asked, putting more food on my plate, pretending not to notice the unfinished pieces that were still there.

I shook my head.

My parents exchanged worried glances and then, after a while, my father spoke. "Collie, there's something we have been wanting to tell you."

I swallowed hard. Oh no, here it comes! I thought of every bad thing that could have happened.

"We're moving."

"Huh?" I knew what he said; I just wanted to pretend he didn't say it, hoping I was wrong. Funny, that wasn't one of the things I thought he might say.

My father looked at my mom nervously and then looked at me, forcing a weak smile. "Bennett and Foresman have opened up a new firm in Boston. And, well . . . they picked me to manage it. Collie, it's the chance of a lifetime, one that I've been waiting for."

I stared. Not at my parents, but down, at my hands. Davis once said, jokingly, that I had beautiful hands. But in a way, I thought he meant it. My hands were sweating now. They were nervous. Davis would have been disappointed.

"Collie?" my mom said, concerned. "It's going to be great, sweetie, I promise. There will be lots of snow. You always loved snow." She was talking to me as if I was a two-year-old. It must have been already determined.

After a couple of unbearable minutes of silence, I opened my mouth but nothing came out. Finally a voice whispered, "Boston? When?"

"We want to have you ready for the second semester, so we want to move during Christmas vacation."

I don't remember who answered me, and I don't remember starting to cry, either. I do recall my mom handing me a pink Kleenex which I refused to accept, and the strained expression on my father's face, as if he'd just ruined my adolescence forever.

"Uh, Mom, I have some homework. Could I . . ."

"Sure, sweetie, go ahead."

I walked slowly to my room and closed the door behind me. Almost instinctively, I picked up the phone by my bed and waited for the person on the other end to make my tears stop.

"Hello?"

"Hello, Davis?"

"Marshall? Hey, what's up?"

I didn't answer. I was thinking.

"Marshall? Everything OK? Marrshhaall!"

"Yeah, everything's cool." I couldn't tell him. I was depressed . . . and scared. "Just wanted to know if you had a game tomorrow."

"Yup. Playing King Memorial. We're gonna get creamed." I already knew that.

"Okay, I was just wondering. Bye."

"Later."

I got up and began to pace. I didn't know how to feel, act, or what to say. It really started to tick me off. I felt a tear form in my eye and quickly brushed it away. When I start to cry, I never can stop. But those stupid tears kept forming, multiplying by the second. They fell down my face, leaving black streaks of mascara under my eyes. Then the crying turned into sobs, deep hard chokes that could not be controlled. I fell onto my bed, buried my head in the pillow, and, still crying, fell asleep.

The next afternoon found Davis and me in my room, engaged in our daily ritual of me doing geometry and Davis copying it. The day had been terrible. I spent most of it trying to avoid my friends and trying not to cry. Davis knew something was wrong, but was smart enough not to ask what it was. I knew I had to tell him, though.

"I'm moving."

"Hmmmm?" He was too caught up in trying to get the altitude length of a right triangle.

"I'm moving."

"Yeah, right."

"Davis," I said angrily, reaching over the bed and slamming the geometry book closed. "I'm serious."

Davis looked at me hard, straight into my eyes.

After what seemed an eternity, he looked down. He knew the truth.

"Where?"

"Boston."

"When?"

"Christmas vacation."

Finally his eyes met mine. The "Davis sparkle" wasn't in them.

"Why?"

I started to feel my heart knot. "It's not my decision."

Davis looked down and pretended to be engrossed in the design of my bedspread. He said nothing, but I knew exactly how he felt. Finally, without looking up, he spoke.

"Boston's pretty cool, I guess. The Red Sox and all. There's gonna be a lot of snow. You can ice-skate a lot." He picked up the geometry book and continued to study.

"Geez, Davis, you sound like my mother." I was getting angry now. He acted like he didn't care.

"Well, geez, Colleen, what do you want me to say? That I'm really glad you're moving so I can hang out with Herman Waltflower? I can't say what I want. I can't say don't go because I know you have to." There was anger and confusion in his eyes. I had never seen him this way. It scared me—he called me Colleen.

"It's not my fault," I said, the tears starting to flow.

"Look, I gotta go now. It's getting late." Davis got up, gathered his things, and without another word, left, slamming the door behind him.

I didn't cry that night. I was too mad—at everybody. At my dad for accepting a job thousands of miles away, at my mom for agreeing to go along with it, at Davis for being such a lousy friend when I needed him most, and at me for being mad and not crying.

The next day I tried to find Davis to talk to him, but at the same time tried to avoid his presence. The first time I saw him was in Mrs. Drew's English class. He didn't look my way, so I tried not to look his. We were studying poetry, and our assignment for the day was to write a list of ten things. God only knows how that is poetry, but I was too preoccupied to think about it. I looked over at Davis to see if he would give me one of his this-is-such-a-stupid-class looks, but he didn't. He just stared straight ahead, very intent on what Mrs. Drew was saying. He didn't talk to me for the rest of the school day.

That afternoon the doorbell rang. I was too busy lying on my bed being depressed to answer it, but then I remembered no one was home. I lazily opened the door.

"Could you help me with geometry? I have no idea what's going on." Davis gave me a shy grin and invited himself inside.

"Davis, I'm sorry. I really shouldn't have . . ."

"Hey, Marshall, forget about it. It's not your fault. I should be the one who's sorry. Boston, huh? No offense, but you're gonna freeze your rear up there."

I laughed. This was the way it should have been.

"Let's not talk about you moving anymore, OK? Promise?"

"Promise."

Davis smiled, satisfied. "So what did you think about Drew's poem today? I wrote ten reasons why the Oilers never made it to the Super Bowl. What a stupid class."

And that was that.

Two months came and went. And as we promised, Davis and I didn't mention anything about moving. He helped me pack, but we never actually discussed why. We went on with our daily routine as if I wasn't leaving: him copying geometry, me watching his football games, him proofreading my newspaper articles.

Then the day before moving day came. We were in my room comparing Christmas presents. We laughed, talked, and gossiped, but we knew the time to say goodbye was coming nearer.

"Uh, well, Merry Christmas," he said, giving me a small wrapped box.

"Thanks," I said, opening the gift. I already gave him my present that morning, which I don't think he really liked—but he did a really good job of acting like he did.

Inside the box was a golden locket. It was beautiful.

"Uh, my mom picked it out because you know how I am with girl presents," he said laughing. "I thought you would like it, though. I didn't put my picture in it 'cause you might find a really cute guy up there in Massachusetts. But there's something engraved in it so you won't forget me."

"Thanks." I immediately put it on. I loved it.

"Oh, here's another thing." He gave me a small

envelope. He smiled. "This is really from me. Don't open it yet, though. After I leave."

I wanted to ask why, but I just nodded obediently.

"Well, I gotta go now. It's getting late." He got up awkwardly and headed for the door. "Boston will be awesome, Marshall. I promise. You'll be fine." He smiled at me.

"Bye."

"Later." Davis opened my bedroom door.

I felt tears running down my face. "I love you, Davis."

He turned around and smiled. His eyes sparkled with little teardrops ready to fall. "I know, Marshall." And with that he walked away.

I closed my door and let the dam break. I sat down on the floor, and through the tears read what Davis had written.

TEN THINGS COLLEEN K. MARSHALL
SHOULD ALWAYS REMEMBER IN BOSTON
1) Don't get one of those gross New England accents.
2) In association with #1, say "ya'll" as much as possible.
3) She's beautiful.
4) Even if she's in Boston, she will always be a Texan at heart.
5) Her name is Marshall.
6) No matter what anyone tells her, she's going to be a writer. She will write only the truth.
7) It's not her fault if a certain person flunks geometry. Ha, Ha.
8) She's not fat, she's not fat, she's not fat.

9) Oilers rule!

10) And the last thing Colleen K. Marshall should always remember in Boston is that even though he never says it, Davis R. Vaughn loves her too.

How could he write this? He knew I would cry. Despite all my tears, I found myself laughing. Laughing at what he wrote and all the good times we had. Davis knew me so well, better than anyone else, and I was leaving him. But as the gold locket said, "We'll always be together."

So here I am in Boston, going to a Catholic private school (thank heaven it's coed), wearing a red plaid uniform I wouldn't be caught dead wearing in Houston, and shoveling snow from my driveway every morning.

The bell rang. I slowly gathered my things from Sister Mary Catherine's literature class and walked out the door. I hadn't made many friends here— well, I really hadn't tried that hard—so it surprised me when I heard someone call my name down the hallway. I turned and saw a guy running toward me, panting.

"Hi, I'm Richard Luis. I'm the editor of the newspaper here. Call me Rick, though."

"Oh, hi. I'm Colleen Marshall. Call me . . ." I thought about it, "Colleen."

"I know." I felt surprised and kind of flattered that he did. "Sister Agnes says you're a very talented writer. We heard that you were on the news staff at your old school . . . in Texas?"

"Yes I was, in Houston."

"Houston, huh? The Oilers are pretty good."

I smiled, choking back a giggle.

"Well, anyway," he continued, "we really need some good writers, so I was wondering if you'd like to be on the staff."

"Yeah, that would be great." I couldn't believe my luck.

"Cool. What do you write?"

I thought of the list of ten things, which reminded me of Davis. "Only the truth."

Loubel Cruz
Klein Forest High School, Houston, Texas

Medium Shots

Stories of school and the community

The Bus Ride

by Kristi Hooper

This year on the bus it's so crowded. I feel suffocated. Sometimes, on rainy, damp mornings when the bus driver has the heat on, I feel like I'm going to go crazy if I don't get some fresh air. The mixture of the heater and dozens of bodies concentrated into that small space is almost unbearable. "Turn off the heat!" yells someone from the back. The bus driver claims the heat must be on for some reason concerning the windshield wipers. I look outside and it rains harder. No hope of opening the window. More people cram on. I am now squished up against the hard, metal side of the bus by two other people wedged into the seat with me. There's hardly room to squirm. And for a moment I imagine what it would feel like to move freely and breathe while on that fifty-minute bus ride. Then the fantasy disappears like the rocks and pebbles flying past me on the road.

Kristi Hooper
Traverse City Jr. High School, Traverse City, Michigan

Lunch

by Noel Allain

W ell, I was leaning against the wall when she came down the hall. She was so hot and looked like . . ."

Tuna fish. I hate tuna fish and Mom always packs it. I was sitting at a lunch table staring at my gruesome lunch while my friend David told me some tale off the top of his head about how some girl he didn't even know came over to him and . . . well, forget it.

"Are you listening to me?"

"What? Oh, no."

"Well, listen. When I went to New York last weekend I met this girl in the lounge, and that night I snuck over to her room and when I opened the door, there was . . ."

Carrots. I hate carrots. Gross! My mother never packs food I like.

"Noel, listen. See that girl over there? Well, I was walking up the stairs today in school and the lights were out. So I hear her whispering my name, and go to where she was and right away she was . . ."

A Yahoo drink box! I hate Yahoo. It tastes like watery chocolate soda. Wait—it *is* watery chocolate soda, man! I never get a good lunch, I thought, as I groaned at David's blabbering.

"Noel, listen to me . . ."

"Shut up, David! Just shut up."

"Noel, what's the difference—my love, your lunch?"

"My lunch is real. Now, like I said: Shut up and eat your peanut butter and jelly."

Noel Allain
Weston Middle School, Weston, Massachusetts

Weight Loss

by Gitte Peng

I smiled sweetly at her chubby face, my eyes soaking in her beaming smile, her squinty eyes, and fat, pink cheeks. She seemed ready to explode. Through gritted teeth, I congratulated her and dismissed her squeaky thanks. She reached out with pudgy white fingers to shake my hand, and when I kept my fists clenched at my sides, she shrugged her shoulders, stuck a puffy thumb between her big, wet lips, and sucked.

I crept away from her, seething, and slunk into my chair by the window.

"Hungry," Sister Frieda had monotoned, "Hungry. Your word, Gertrude."

With an air of content, Gertrude spelled, "Hungry. H-U-N-G-R-Y. Hungry."

"Very good. The next word is weight," the nun said slowly. "Weight as in pounds, how much a person weighs." She nodded at me expectantly. "Your word." Only Gertrude and I were still standing. Everyone else had been eliminated.

I hesitated and drew in my breath, for I was unfamiliar with this word. However, I did recall that it was a "G-H-T" word and pleaded with my mind to give me the other letters. "Weight," I almost whispered, hardly daring to speak, "W-A-I-G-H-T. Weight."

Sister Frieda shook her head apologetically. "No, that is incorrect, dear." My heart sank.

"Now, Gertrude, if you can spell it right, you will be our new spelling bee champion. The word is weight, as in pounds, how much a person weighs."

The first-grade class sat still in its stiffly-starched uniforms, waiting for the unpopular and fat Gertrude Bunt to spell the word. I bit my lip and tried to cease the shaking in my legs. She twitched and rubbed her hands on her stomach, then grinned.

"Weight. W-E-I-G-H-T. Weight."

"You are correct! Excellent job!" exclaimed the Sister with a broad smile. "You are the new spelling bee champion, Miss Bunt!"

My stomach knotted as the class clapped for her. That was *my* applause! That was my name on the bulletin board for all to see. They couldn't take it down!

"Shake hands now, girls," directed Sister Frieda, removing my bee-shaped construction paper from the board to make room for a new one. I did not want to shake Gertrude's hand. I wanted to hit her. I had been champion for the past five weeks—defeating everyone else. Now Gertrude Bunt had beaten me. Gertrude Bunt.

Holding back a flood of tears, I grimaced at how unfair it was to let Gertrude spell that word. Why, weight was her whole life. She had probably been hearing the word since she was born! She weighed so much, there was no way she could have gotten it wrong. How could a thirty-five-pound kid like me be expected to know about weight?

Gertrude alternately sucked on her thumb and the lollipop she had received as her prize. I knew there was no justice in this place. I knew that my name was no longer on the bulletin board. I knew that I had been faced with my first loss.

In the spelling bee that day, I learned to spell two new words, and the second was one I had never expected I would have to know—defeat.

Gitte Peng
Dulaney High School, Timonium, Maryland

Weston Library

by Andrew Nozik

There I was, sitting with my pals in the corner of the library, all of us holding some book that we picked up from the shelf so we could look busy. I was starting a report about King Arthur and his Knights of the Round Table, when She walked in. The sunlight glimmered off her shiny brown hair. I thought to myself that she couldn't be from Weston. She was way too pretty. The way she glanced around, studying every little minute detail of the front hall, gave away that she hadn't been here before. She almost bumped into the card catalog in the center of the room. I always thought it was a silly place for it.

"Yo, guys, look who just walked in." My voice, low and solid, came out leisurely and forced them to look. Why I always tell them everything is beyond me. Three years, I've told them everything; why'd I tell them this? They all looked. She gracefully turned from the card catalog, looked in our direction and smiled. Her moist lips tightened as the skin stretched back into a small semicircle. I thought my eyes were playing tricks on me, fooling me into thinking that she was prettier than she really was. My left thumb itched with anticipation. Okay, keep cool. Relax. Nothing embarrassing will happen. Just stay cool.

She started to walk over to us. Her hips swayed from side to side. You could tell something was going to happen. She had deep, dark brown eyes that matched her hair. Beauty was almost near. My group started acting like wild boars, and one almost grunted. Ace even went so far as to whistle at her.

She came up to the table, looked around, and sat in an empty chair next to mine. She looked at me with a peculiar expression. Our eyes met. Mine flashed back to the herd. Each one of them was staring right back at me. I looked at her again. No one said anything. As always, I was the one who started things up.

I could see now that the skin on her face was smooth, soft, and silky. I could smell her perfume drifting over the piles of books between us on the table and lingering in the space in front of me. By now my thumb throbbed in pain, as I had all I could do to keep from scratching it.

The tension in our corner of the room felt as if it would explode. Alex had laid down his book and just sat there open-mouthed, staring at her. Beauty kept her cool. I could tell she had dealt with situations like this before. It seemed as if the whole library had dropped what it was doing and was looking at us. Ted shrank back in his seat and became smaller. The herd was whimpering. They fell to her power, as they had to mine. If the bus hadn't come so early this morning, I might have had time to rehearse my well-known lines of "What ya doin' after school today?" or, "Do you want to go to the Center?"

Tom almost bowed to her as if he were her personal slave, and Jake was close to yelping in horror as her gaze pierced through him. They googooed as she flicked her brown hair with her delicate hand. The raising of my right eyebrow at her, however, pushed them back into their seats and kept them there. Sam dropped his book on medieval knights and totally forgot about his research paper, which was already late. Beauty and I seemed to share this power over people. I don't know if it made us superior or if they were simply weaker, but either way, I liked it.

Beauty was relaxing by leaning back and letting the two front legs of her chair lift off the floor. But wait a minute . . . why is she looking at Tom? Doesn't she know that he is the stupidest one here? Look at that dumb look on his face. He can't even do an addition problem without a calculator. She might consider Freddie if he would open his mouth and say something. Or Jack might win her hand if he wouldn't fool around so much and actually think.

But not to worry—I was King! I knew all of them better than they knew themselves, could anticipate their every move. Yes, I had mastered them. And she knew it. She turned back to me. King Arthur and his Queen were on their thrones; peasants would have to beg for mercy! The library was our castle, and Weston our kingdom.

Andrew Nozik
Weston Middle School, Weston, Massachusetts

My First Word

by Steve Smith

A baby's first word is one of the most important and happy memories a parent can have. Unfortunately, my parents' memories of my first word aren't all happy!

It all started when we were living in Illinois. I was about eighteen months old, and I had just started saying my first word. I know I meant it to be "truck" because every time one went by I would shout a word that sounded like "truck." But to everyone else it sounded like something one would find on the bathroom wall of a gas station.

My parents tried to get me to say it right, but I couldn't. Finally, they gave up and hoped I'd get it right when I got older. About three months later, we packed up to move to Virginia. As we waited for our plane in O'Hare International Airport, which happens to be the largest airport in the world, I ambled over to a huge window overlooking the runway. At that very moment, a luggage cart was driving across the runway, its many trailers rattling behind. It was the largest truck in the world! I had to tell someone about this! I turned to my father, who was standing next to about a thousand people waiting for various flights, and screamed, "DADDY, DADDY!!! %*$#¢!!! %*$#¢!!!!!"

My father desperately tried to shut me up, but I was so excited I kept screaming my special word. My poor mother decided she didn't know this disgusting toddler and ran into the ladies' room, where she hid until I finally stopped. Even now, thirteen years later, there are probably hundreds of people who were at the airport that day still wondering what that little boy actually saw outside.

Well, I learned how to say "truck" correctly, and soon I was talking like a normal kid. However, my parents will never forget the incident at O'Hare.

Steve Smith
West Springfield High School, Springfield, Virginia

An Eerie Night

by Stephen Leroy

W*hoosh!* The meteor zoomed across the sky and landed somewhere in the woods of our backyard. My friend Dave and I got out of bed and rushed out, ignoring my mother calling us.

We had seen the meteor through my window. Suddenly we saw a faint glow. As we moved toward the meteor, the light grew brighter. I yelled for Dave to go get a bucket of water. He came back and the meteor was glowing more than ever. We dumped water on the thing, and it seemed to be smiling. We heard a loud crack, and the meteor split in half. Then we saw millions of bugs covering the meteor. Dave and I were too frozen to move. The bugs began crawling up Dave's arm and into his hair. I heard a piercing scream and Dave was lying on the ground, dead.

I ran and didn't stop until I got to our house. I got my father and a jar. We both ran out to see Dave, but when we got to that spot, there was nothing to be seen. No bugs, no meteor, no Dave. But then out of the trees came Dave. He was alive! There were no marks on him. He said, "Why did you run away? I lost the flashlight."

"What flashlight?" I asked. "We didn't have a flashlight."

"How can you play flashlight tag without a flashlight?" he asked.

"But—"

My father interrupted me. "Let's go home, boys."

"Wait!" I yelled. I grabbed the jar and scooped up what I saw.

"That's a louse," my dad said.

Dave yelled, "No!" Just then all the bugs started to leave Dave's head. They left through his nose, his mouth, ears, and hair. I screamed as loud as I could, which was the most embarrassing thing that ever happened to me.

Every head in the class turned and laughed as Ms. Avery sent me to the office for dozing off in class.

That night a meteor passed my window. I hid under my covers and went to sleep.

Stephen Leroy
Middlesex Middle School, Darien, Connecticut

My Last Chance

by Zahra Marvi

I really have to go now, Wendy," says Judy. Judy's my best friend.

"OK, bye."

It is the last day of school. The last day of the eighth grade. And I'm just standing here, waiting for the school bus to come. Well, I guess it will be the last time I get to ride it. Next year I'll have to take the subway to Stuyvesant. I still can't believe I made it. I turn around to look at him. I can't believe he didn't! If you are wondering who "he" is, "he" is Jim. I have had a huge crush on him since the beginning of the year.

My friends told me that I should ask him out, but I don't want to take the chance. What is taking this bus so long? It is so boring standing out here all alone. Everyone is leaving. Maybe I should talk to him. What can I say?

"Hi, Jim."

Silence.

He didn't even hear me! Here comes Melanie. Jim asks her to wait and says something to her which I can't hear.

"OK, so I'll give you a call. Bye, says Melanie. Then she walks off.

Wow! I don't even feel comfortable saying 'Hi' to this guy and she is going to give him a call! Where did I go wrong?

Then Jenny comes along. "Hey, everyone. I heard the bus won't be coming, so you better find some other way to get home."

Oh, well. I'll just walk home. A few steps down the street and I realize I am not alone—Jim is walking in the same direction! He must be going to his aunt's house. She lives in my building!

So now we are walking together. What should I do? Should I try talking again? I never really talked to him before. Why should I start now? We will be there pretty soon. Why is he walking so fast?

I finally get enough courage to say something. "Hi! Are you going to your aunt's house?"

"Yes," he says, turning to me. He is so cute! We walk on in silence. I can't think of anything else to say to him. Before I know it, we're there.

The doorman opens the door for us and we enter the building. Jim rushes ahead of me. When I get to the elevator, he's holding the door for me.

"Thank you," I say.

He presses eight. I press nine. We are all alone in the elevator! OK. If I ask him out now, what is the worst thing he can say? He can say no. And I'll never have to face him again.

"Oh, I was wondering . . . ooo," we both say at the same time.

"What did you want to say?" he asks.

"Oh . . . Never mind. You?" I wonder what he

wanted to say to me.

"Um, never mind," he says. The door opens and he gets off.

"Bye," I call loudly.

"Bye, Wendy." The door closes behind him.

Zahra Marvi
Wagner Jr. High School 167, New York, New York

The Old Man

by Brian Williams

The old man was tired. As he bent over the hoe in the old garden, one could see that he was exhausted from working in the hot sun. Sweat dripped from the folds of his chin as he moved the hoe back and forth, back and forth, like a pendulum on a clock. He paused to eject a stream of tobacco juice through his loose front teeth. He looked at the sun and felt the heat penetrate the loose skin of his face. He went back to the job at hand. As he moved down the row of corn, he limped on his bad leg. He walked like a dog with three legs. He could tell that he was getting too old for this job. The hoe was getting heavier; the rows were getting longer. He began to feel dizzy. He stood up, but he could not maintain his balance any longer. He fell to the ground in a heap. No one could even tell that he was there, for his clothes were the color of the ground. The man finally rested.

Brian Williams
Meadville Sr. High School, Meadville, Pennsylvania

The Schoolroom

by Shannon Goodall

The walls, funny how we never notice them. The paint, carefully chosen, is always a calm color. Whipped blue, creamy green, warm milk, lemon pudding. Too quiet. The teachers make it louder. Construction paper, the brightest you can buy, spells out something on the wall. Bulletin boards, some simple with a message, others educational; the best are personal. Posters with cute sayings live on the walls; you get to know them. When you're bored or stumped, these walls become your friends.

The bookshelves are covered with books without titles. They form repetitive patterns—a red stripe, green scribbles on black.

The clock over the door makes its double click sound, reminding you that you still are.

The people you know sit evenly spaced around the room. Each one in a calm-colored chair (no, I think they're just cheap-colored), resting their arms, like my own, on a false wood desk top. Black and gold short skirts . . . must be a football game tonight, maybe volleyball.

The bell rings. Suddenly it's loud; laughing, yell-ing, swearing. The peace is lost.

Shannon Goodall
Horning Middle School, Waukesha, Wisconsin

My Brother, My Heart

by Nancy O'Neale

I sang with the choir as they led the church into the hymn. I so much wanted to be a choir member, to be in the bliss unison, but I believed I never would. My brother, my best friend, stuttered, and I could never be so cruel as to leave him and sit with the people in the loft. It was a mistake for me to even be singing. This was Riley's most nervous time in the church service. To block out the noise of the choir, I examined the celestial building and all the people in it. It had five, six— no, seven stained glass windows. The light shone through the apse in the summer. The benches were of hard maple wood. My brother and I were sitting between my grandmother and mother. The people in the loft were now in their seats. The preacher took his stand behind the sturdy pulpit.

"Time to go to sleep," I whispered to my brother.

"Ree-Ree, hush your mouth!" hissed my stone-faced mother.

The pastor had started his sermon. "God is no respecter of persons." I thought he preached this same sermon last week. It seemed like he preached the same sermon every week. Either that or the whole

Bible blended in together. As soon as we left the wooden edifice I knew my mother would not forget my misbehavior of speaking in church.

"For your disobedience both of you will walk home."

Even Mama must have perceived that this was more of a blessing than a punishment. Riley and I enjoyed taking long walks. Our distances were challenging and we always tried to discover new territory. My brother and I held hands as we started the mile-long journey, which was about the same as the distance to school. We stepped over plenty of rocks, *crush, stomp, crush, stomp,* on the dirt road and hardly spoke. When we reached home my stockings were a bit discolored, but my brother remained spotless. We sat down on the worn-out porch, licking cherry-lemonade Popsicles and watching my grandmother sway in her rocking chair while sipping her tart-tasting lemonade.

The next morning, like all mornings, Greenville woke up to a chilling dew-mist instead of sun. The coldness of the bitter dawn was hard to suffer for my brother and me as we walked the mile to school. We didn't hold hands. He said that only Sunday should be reserved for showing affection. I worried that it might make me look less than my seventeen years to be walking with a little kid and holding his hand, but I never told him this.

Even though I was an honor student, beyond boredom, I felt resentment during classes. If God is no respecter of persons, then why did the Negro schools have secondhand books and the white kids receive new books with fresh covers and uncut pages?

Why were some sick and some well? Why were few rich and most poor? That's what we were, dirt poor. Although my mother often camouflaged it, the fact of our indigence still remained. My crisp-ironed, homemade dresses and my brother's clean striped suit did not make up for the frequent greens and cornbread dinners. If God is no respecter of persons, then how come my brother stuttered and I spoke clearly? Before my thoughts were finished we had arrived at school.

After school it was time to walk over the tarred concrete and behind the fence to the elementary section where I picked up Riley. My brother dashed out of his seat to hug me.

"Why are you so excited, Riley?"

"I saw s-snow!"

What! He saw snow. One thing I knew is that it never snowed in Greenville, or, if it had, it hadn't snowed today. The dawns were bitter cold but the vermilion dirt in the afternoon was enough to make the soles of your shoes melt.

"It doesn't snow in Greenville, Riley," I retorted.

"I uh-know that," he said matter-of-factly. "We-we saw a m-m-movie in c-c-class on-on-on nature!" He stopped to take a breath. "It's the most bu-bu-bu-beautiful stuff I've ever s-s-s-seen!"

I doubted that he'd ever see snow unless a storm came to Greenville. My grandmother and mother were born here and they never left. They'd been to Savannah a couple of times to pick peaches to make peach nectar and peach jam. I wondered if Riley would ever leave Greenville. I hoped to receive a scholarship from some small black college. My father lived in Chicago. He would never allow Riley to visit. He didn't want any handicapped children; he considered Riley's stuttering a handicap. I'd seen snow a couple of times.

"I wa-wa-wanna s-s-see some snow!"

Now he was whining. He hadn't whined since he was a baby and I couldn't stand it then. Riley was not my full responsibility. Momma would have to take care of this.

"We'll talk to Momma when we get home," I said in a restrained voice.

We took the path home that we had recently discovered. Riley babbled as well as he could about the snow. I kept saying that we would discuss it with Mother. The silence of the bronze earth was much as it was on Sunday afternoon. The heat only changed with the seasons, except for an occasional rainfall.

A car slowing alongside us soon broke the silence. They had their convertible top down. Riley was on the outside of me and they might try to spit on him. I pulled him over and we switched sides. *Crunch, stomp, crunch, stomp,* our pace increased. They continued to follow with snickers and chuckles among them. One white leaned out of a car door.

"N-N-N-Nigger!"

The word rang in my mind. I reached into the bronze earth and picked up what lay there. I threw it with all my strength. The car was a little way in front of us and I hit that white boy in the back of his blond head. The rock had been my friend. The tawny dust had been a companion.

"You-you-you-you h-h-hit him, R-Ree! You hit him!"

The snickers turned into shock as they sped away. Curiosity had risen in me: How did that white boy know my brother stuttered? I knew the remark was targeted more to my brother than me. We couldn't tell Momma about this.

"We're going to find a different route to school," was all I said. My brother was still rejoicing when suddenly he ceased.

"Why did they c-c-c-call me a n-n-n-nigger?" Incredulous concern mixed with the cracked impairment that would never heal. "I-I c-can't help it if I-I-I'm a nigger!"

"Oh, Riley, you're not a nigger. You are not a nigger . . ."

I held my brother tight. I had to keep myself strong so that he wouldn't fall apart. I walked the rest of the way home asking myself how to explain racism and bigotry to a seven-year-old, knowing we'd be embraced by it for the rest of our lives.

Later that night Riley came into my room while I was sleeping. He had a temper tantrum.

"I wa-wanna see some s-s-snow! I wa-wa-wanna see some s-s-snow! . . ." At his every demand he made a crescendo of uproar.

I thought about slapping him into silence but I knew I could never hit my brother. I'd promised Riley he'd discuss the snow this evening with his momma. Where was his mother, anyway? Always working, always working. Couldn't she take time to raise her children? Why couldn't he leave me alone!

"Riley, be quiet before you wake Grandmother! I told you it doesn't snow in Greenville."

"I can go ta Chi-Chi-Chi-cago! You went ta Chi-

Chi-Chi-cago! I can h-h-h-hitchhike," he grimaced.
"I know my d-d-daddy loves me jus-just as much as
he loves you!"

I couldn't believe he was comparing me to himself. He didn't understand that Dad was a respecter
of persons. I rose out of my bed.

"You hitchhike, boy, and you're going to come
back with a rope around your neck hanging on a
tree."

"I-I'm gonna pack now, to start my t-trip . . ." He
had a rascally grin on his face as if he had out-
smarted me. I caught him by his pajama sleeve and
dragged him to the kitchen where his voice echoed. I
opened the icebox to let my head cool off and took
out the cherry-lemonade Popsicles because I knew
they were his favorite. I don't know what I planned
to do with the Popsicles. Maybe I was going to suc-
cor my brother, as if giving candy to a baby.

Instead, I yanked the toothpicks out of the ice
trays, emptying the trays onto our good wooden cut-
ting board. I searched for the potato masher in the
silverware drawer and crushed the Popsicles . . . I
was going to give him some snow, alright! I scooped
it all up and then threw the crushed ice into his face.
My grandmother was standing in the kitchen doorway. She picked up her plump "picking" hand and
slapped me hard. The right side of my sheepish face
throbbed. Numbness, just like my frozen fingers.

"Clean up this mess and go to bed!" she bellowed.

"Yes, ma'am," I whispered.

Why was I the one to be slapped? Why did I have
to suffer the consequences when my brother was the

one who was so stubborn and annoying? I heard water running in the bathroom and I knew Riley was washing his face for the second time tonight. I felt a bitter hatred for my brother, for that white boy, for everyone.

This just wasn't fair. I was seventeen and had never even been to the movies. I wanted to be in the church choir. I wanted friends to go to the ice cream parlor with. I wanted a normal life and I didn't want a brother who stuttered. The word "stutter" made me shiver.

The air in the kitchen became too thin. I took off my nightgown, put on a crisp-ironed white dress, and went through the back door to the side of the house. I started to shake and shiver without a sound from my mouth. Stuffy tears came out into the darkness, striking the tawny dust and coloring it vermilion. I wanted to reshape my life in this clay. I rolled around in the yellow-red substance until my dress was fully dirty. I chased all the virtue out of me, and now I was satisfied. Once back in my shelter, my bedroom, I took off my moist, wrinkled dress and climbed into bed. I didn't even wash my face.

Nancy O'Neale
Wayland Academy, Beaver Dam, Wisconsin

Wide Angles

Stories of nature and the human spirit

If I Were a Gentle Wind

by Brad Phillips

If I were a gentle wind, I would rise in the morning before the sparrows begin to sing. I would dance freely on the mist-covered lakes. My great body would fly gracefully across the plains and mountains, and glide swiftly between the trees of the deep evergreen forest. I would get up with the loons and dance to their heavenly sounds as they echoed across the lake. If I were a gentle wind, I would float across the meadows and stop to say hi to all the animals. I might carry a great bird such as an eagle on my strong back and send him on his way. There would be no place I couldn't go or see. Every lake, every forest, just a breath away. My body would never tire and my muscles would never tense. Every mile I would fly would seem like inches. I would be the most unhindered thing on earth, and that is all it would take to please me.

Brad Phillips
Rippon Middle School, Woodbridge, Virginia

Freedom

by Joanne Adamkewicz

I fly on winged feet down dusty paths. I soar over fallen logs, jumping higher and higher. I crane my neck to gaze intently at the patterns of light squeezing through the maze of leaves. I stop under the boughs of a mighty pine and imagine that I stand in a grand cathedral. A dusty-looking sunbeam tickles my toes. Birds call out wild hellos to my straining ears.

Then I take off again, traveling to my favorite haunts and dancing across a field, pretending it is my stage. I take a daring leap across the wide stream bed and laugh at the water yearning to get me. A hickory-bark boat with a brave, yellow dandelion pennant leaves port to sail the uncharted depths of the stream. As I watch it go, I exult in my freedom . . .

With a disappointed sigh, I face reality. The wishes don't work. The wheelchair is still here, and I am still its prisoner.

Joanne Adamkewicz
Rocky Run Intermediate School, Chantilly, Virginia

Déjà Vu

by Carmen Nobel

All the children had arrived, so the Sunday school teacher began the story. She was reading from the *New Children's Bible,* a book which made the Bible interesting and easy to understand for the children. She sometimes read from the *First Children's Bible,* but the children seemed to like the stories from the New better.

"Once there was a man," began the teacher, when she saw a child's hand go up.

"What, Luella?" She smiled patiently.

"Is this a true story?" the child asked.

"Yes," said the teacher. "All of the stories from the *New Children's Bible* are true. We know that for a fact."

She continued. "The man's name was Noah, and he was a good man. God loved Noah but, unfortunately, he felt that Noah was the only good man. God felt there was only one thing to do. He called Noah one day."

"On the teph-alone?" a child asked.

The teacher ignored this. "God told Noah that there would be a great destruction in which everyone would die. But God told Noah that if he followed His directions, Noah wouldn't die.

"First Noah had to build a ship. This ship would save him and his family. Then Noah had to collect two of each kind of animal on the Earth. They were to go on the ship, too. God wanted all of them to start a new world after everyone else had died.

"Noah did what God told him to, and soon God called him again: 'Now is the time, Noah,' He bellowed.

"And Noah and all the animals hurried into the ship. The ship was launched. Noah looked out of the ship and saw . . . well, what do you think he saw, children?"

"A lot of rain?" a boy asked.

"No, Raymond, that's in the *First Children's Bible*. That was another Noah. This Noah saw the Earth below him. He saw two explosions and two mushroom-shaped clouds. The great destruction had begun. Noah would have to find a new place to live." The teacher closed the book.

"And that's why we live here, teacher, and not on Earth, right?" Luella asked.

"That's right."

Carmen Nobel
Gorham High School, Gorham, Maine

Benediction

by Tricia Crockett

The weariness in my body pushes me to sleep, but my heart is thinking many thoughts.

Indians are one soul. We learn through the old, who have known the soul of the earth the longest. The earth has the oldest soul of all.

My inside self sings loudly when the ground is decorated with water, bringing it life. It's often hard to hold it inside so that I don't show how happy I am.

But by the fireside, you can see my soul dance with happiness in the shadows.

I'm the happiest, though, when the sun sets the cliffs on fire and warms the stones from the cold of night. The sheep laugh as they walk up the path. The land is clean and wonderful. My soul answers the earth's soul when it speaks like this, hoping for praise.

We talk without a human word. But we say, *I am Indian*. My veins pump with the same red clay of the hills. My baby sleeps the quiet sleep of the mountains and becomes strong. The land is my friend.

Without her, I die.

Tricia Crockett
Oyster River High School, Durham, New Hampshire

Anonomatos*

by Owen Thomas

I was 20 years old when I met the dragon. Villagers had reported seeing a thing flying overhead at night; fires had started mysteriously in the fields; and a young boy declared that he had seen a dragon crawling into a cave in the hills.

Despite my youth, I was chosen by the village to find the dragon and deal with it. Normally, a more experienced knight would have been sent, but they had gone to fight in the latest border war.

The boy who had seen the dragon led me to where he had seen it. Clothed in armor and armed with a sword, I entered the cave.

I did not expect to find anything: in truth, I thought that the villagers' imaginations were simply running wild. There had been no reports of dragons for 40 or 50 years. At night, a flock of birds could seem like a dragon. It had been a dry summer, and it would not be difficult to start a fire through carelessness. As for the boy—boys dream.

What I saw in that cave took me by surprise: I saw a dragon.

The dragon was not the foul, serpentine creature

that had always been described to me. This dragon
was more akin to a cloud or a rainbow: ethereal,
shifting, beautiful. She (for somehow I know it was
she) glowed with a pure white radiance that was not
of earth but rather of her soul; it outlined her form,
making indistinct that which I doubted was even
there.

And she said to me, "You have come to kill me,
child."

It was not a question. She knew. I could feel her
inside my mind, seeing my thoughts.

"Why?" she asked.

I could not reply.

"Do you know what I am, child?"

I shook my head mutely.

"Child, you cannot kill me, any more than you
can extinguish the stars glowing in the sky. I am a
part of nature. When I fly, I am a cloud, drifting
slowly, pushed by the winds; in the water, I am a
wave, swelling, breaking against the rocks and re-
treating, over and over again; and when I breathe
fire—for yes, I do breathe fire, as your legends say—
I am the angry heat, a swiftly darting flicker of
flame."

I knew then what she was, Spirit of Fire, Air, and
Water, beside which I was nothing, beside which I
was helpless. She was a raging fire, a hurricane gale,
a mighty wave; yet she was also a living warmth, a
gentle breeze, a shimmering ripple.

"Child, you cannot blame me for what I do any
more than you could assail Mother Nature herself.
Tell those who sent you here what you please; they
shall not see any more dragons. They shall find an-

other reason for their troubles: let them blame the wind, let them curse the water, let them fault the fire. Dragons are too easy an excuse.

"No, child, they shall see no more dragons, but I shall remain. Search for me."

She faded from my sight, but as she had said, she was not gone. I felt her in the wind that whistled between the trees, I heard her in the gentle lapping of waves by the shore, and I saw her in the soft flickering of the fire.

When I returned to the village, I said that the dragon was gone. But I knew—just as she had told me—that that could never be.

* "Of the One Without a Name" (Greek derivative).

Owen Thomas
Thomas Jefferson High School for Science and Technology, Alexandria, Virginia

Stupid

by Gerard Golden

Sometimes I wish I were stupid. And I don't mean your everyday kid who fails tests here and there or even classes here and there. I mean really stupid, beyond repair. A real idiot. Then I wouldn't have to worry about the earth suddenly losing its force of gravity and drifting out into space where I'd suffocate and die. I wouldn't even know what gravity is.

I wouldn't think twice before getting into the passenger seat of a car late at night, wouldn't wonder if I had a faulty seat belt or if there was a drunk driver around the corner, or if the fumes from the car in front of me were coming in through my window and giving me cancer. I'd be a drunk driver myself and be too bombed to care about my safety.

I wouldn't feel guilty throwing out the leftovers of my huge helping of turkey on Thanksgiving, mindless of the people starving in Somalia and others within miles who are dreaming of getting just a taste. I would not have even heard of Planet Somalia and I wouldn't understand why they couldn't just go to the drive-thru at the local McDonald's.

I wouldn't worry about school tests and term papers and have terrible insomnia every night—because I would fail them all, and then fall into beautifully deep dreamland.

Gerard Golden
Clarkstown High School North, New City, New York

I Am Kwakkoli

by Bisco Hill

Afew months after my tenth birthday, my dad began to talk to me about receiving my Indian name. He said this had to be done in a ceremony by a medicine person or an elder in our tribe. My older sister, Megan, had received her Indian name, Maquegquay (Woman of the Woods), when she was only three. At that time my family lived on the Oneida Reservation just outside of Green Bay, Wisconsin. My grandfather was alive then, and he asked a medicine man friend of his to name her and made the arrangements. I always thought my sister's Indian name was so perfect for her. I was told the medicine man meditated for three days before the name came to him.

My family moved from Wisconsin to Colorado three years before I was born. My grandfather died when I was only two and a half, and both of these major events delayed my Naming Ceremony. My dad talked about naming me for several years, but it was hard to pull it together long distance. Because of the sacred and traditional aspects of this, it is not like anyone can just call and order a Naming Ceremony, like ordering a pizza! As it happened, my

Uncle Rick became the chairman of the tribe when I was ten, and he was able to talk to the right people and select the time. The right time was the summer solstice, near June 20, and it was also the time of the annual Strawberry Ceremony.

There are many traditions connected to the Naming Ceremony. For one thing, there are a limited number of names among the Oneida people. When a person dies, their name returns to the "pool" of available names and can be given to someone else. The medicine person decides whose energy fits which available name, or a person may ask for a certain name. In my case, I was named after my grandfather through my Anglo name, but I also wanted to take his Indian name, which was available and had been waiting for me for seven years. I felt that if I had both of his names, it made a full circle and I was wholly connected to him and to my family. The name that was his is "Kwakkoli," or "Whippoorwill" in English.

A few days before the ceremony in June of 1990, my parents and I flew to the Oneida Reservation. A friend of my dad made me a beautiful "ribbon shirt." It was a shade of deep turquoise stitched with pink, purple and green ribbons. My family and I thought it was very special and that I looked good in it.

Two days before I was given my Indian name, my Uncle Rick, my dad and I drove around and looked at certain landmarks on the Oneida Reservation. I saw where my dad had grown up. There is a statue in the middle of the reservation of my great-grandmother, Dr. Rosa Minoka Hill. She was the first female Indian physician in the United States.

Oneida is very small and different from any other
city I have known. It has only one school, several
baseball fields, a small convent, a store, a post office,
two churches, three cemeteries, a tribal building, and
about twenty houses. My dad and his brother knew
the names of everyone. They knew who was married
to whom and who everyone's grandparents and parents were. They remembered all kinds of funny stories and laughed a lot. I thought it must be nice to
live in a small town where everyone knows everyone
for all those years. It is also a place where everyone
is connected by common heritage, customs and beliefs.

The night before the ceremony, I got very nervous. My stomach hurt as if I had the flu, but I think
it was just butterflies. I finally fell asleep at about
3:30 in the morning. I don't know what I was afraid
of—maybe just not knowing what was going to happen or what I would have to do. My mother could
not come to the ceremony because only tribal mem-
bers were allowed. We had just learned about this
and I was upset that she couldn't come. She was disappointed, but told me to remember the details and
tell her about it later.

After getting about four hours of sleep, I woke up
to the sound of a shower running. I quickly put on
my ribbon shirt, a pair of black pants and moccasins.
The ceremony was set for 9:30 that morning, so we
had to hurry.

On our short drive to the reservation, my stomach felt like it was going to explode! I had to at least
get those butterflies flying in formation! I was pretty
anxious, but really excited about getting my Indian

name. We arrived at the longhouse a little early and I sat with my dad and one of his friends while other people finished setting up tables and chairs.

The ceremony finally began. The Faithkeeper called up the three clans of the Oneida Tribe: the Bear, the Turtle and the Wolf. I am in the Turtle Clan, so I would be named in the second group. The Faith-keeper named all the children in the Bear Clan, then moved on to the Turtles. He named two people, then stepped in front of me. He spoke to me in Oneida. It is a language with unusual sounds like no other language I have ever heard. Most of the words were not understandable to me. He later translated them as: "You must try to learn the Oneida language and our ways. I would like you to come to some of the other ceremonies and events. You now have an Oneida name, 'Kwakkoli,' and the Creator will know you by that name." I was proud to have both my grandfather's names because he was an important man in our tribe.

The Faithkeeper named the others and we all sat down as the Chief said a few more prayers. After about an hour, we all danced to Indian songs and drum music. It was fun, but it became tiring after a while.

Next, we ate and drank. One of the drinks was a kind of strawberry juice. It is sacred and part of the ceremony because the Creator gave this gift of the strawberry to the Oneida people. The drink was very good.

When it was time to go, we thanked the Faithkeeper and the Chief and gave them gifts. The gift that I received, and will be mine for life, is a very special name that runs through my family and connects me to my grandfather, whom I barely knew. My name also reminds me of the many traditions and beliefs that are part of my heritage and about which I have a lot to learn and understand. I look forward to visiting my reservation as I grow up.

Bisco Hill
Southern Hills Middle School, Boulder, Colorado

The New Year

by Brian Trusiewicz

A sea of gray clouds washed across a gray sky, which wasn't unusual—far from it—but it did seem strange to me at the time. I had looked at a gray sky my entire life, had never seen the sky a different color, yet the scene felt like an anachronism, as if I were an alien gazing upon some alien world of ages past. Before me lay a barren landscape of desert and rusting buildings, something which I was quite used to looking at also, yet strange emotions churned through me. Not depression, nor anger or hatred, but a profound state of equanimity to which I am unaccustomed. I was looking for a sign, and suddenly there appeared in the sky a bird, a beautiful black raven. With emotion tight in my chest I called out, "There is hope!"

Then I woke up. To my real world.

The house was unusually still, for my parents and sisters were asleep, exhausted from the New Year's party the previous night. I had gone to bed early feeling quite depressed, which was my usual disposition. "Live a little!" the people at the party had said to me. Everyone was celebrating, for it was 2100, a centennial! Why celebrate? I slipped on my oxygen mask and stepped outside into the blistering hot air. I looked at the sky, the ugly, wretched sky, but saw no bird. There were no birds, not around here. Birds were the last animals on earth besides humans and dogs, yet people still hunted them. All creatures had been killed off by hunting, pollution, or war, and yet hunters went on hunting. There were perhaps a hundred birds left, scattered around the world.

Why then do we continue to destroy nature? Because we too are dying. And death loves company. I stand outside in the suffocating heat often, and have quite a reputation for eccentricity, but I don't care. Almost everyone goes to the Complex, where there are movies and other forms of entertainment. But I stand here, day after day, bearing silent witness.

The dark clouds roll across the sky like machines of death. Once when I was younger, I saw the ocean, and its image has never left me. Dead. It was dead, its surface swirling with oil. I remember reading about how the sky and ocean had once been blue, a brilliant blue! I can't imagine it, and when I ask other people if they can picture this dream-like fantasy they just smile and say it was never actually blue, never really beautiful. Once, when I started to argue that point, my parents told me that I should think of the sky the way it is now because thinking of it as once being beautiful was too depressing. True, but I think of it anyway. Funny, for years people had been deaf to the warnings, oblivious to the environment they were destroying. Now, people are just deluding themselves, saying that nature had never really been beautiful, never truly magnificent.

However, it's not really so strange, for it's always been human nature to hide from responsibility. "It can never happen to me," they said. Well, it didn't happen to them because they're all dead! The people who ignored the warnings and prophecies are dead and don't have to live through the hell which they created. I do.

I can't help my cynical attitude. If I had lived earlier, I would have wanted to scream at the ignorance. But I'm alive now, and the damage has already been done. Standing here looking at this wasteland, I can see what the whole world looks like: a vulture's paradise. Yes, I know what a vulture is, for I have read much literature of the past. The literature of today might as well be condensed into one book under the title: Hope. For hope is what all the writers are alluding to, hope is what they are saying. Long ago, writers preached, "Correct the problems now before it's too late!" Now they tell us there is still hope! Funny. Forests are dead, animals are dead, we have a very limited water supply, organically grown food is diminishing, yet it's still funny in a twisted sort of way. We laugh to hide from the truth. People spend all of their time at the Complex because they can't face it. Maybe watching movies and hiding from the truth through other forms of entertainment is the best thing we can do, for we're going to die anyway. Nature gave birth to us, and we killed our own mother. I suppose I should try to enjoy whatever enjoyments we have left, but I am addicted, emotionally, to this same scene of death, standing, looking at the desert for hours. I want to scream, but there's no point to it.

The damage is done.

In fourth grade I wrote a paper telling what I did over the summer: "I spent my time outside looking at the land and dreaming of a better land and I know it's a stupid thing to do but it's the only thing I can do because if I don't dream I'll want to die." I don't think I've ever seen a stranger look on a teacher's face. Funny. Even back in grade school I was a semi-depressed misanthrope. I feel just like the land before me looks. In high school I wrote a similar paper and my teacher gave me an F and told me I was unimaginative. Ha! Emotionally burned-out, yes. Unimaginative, no. I must have been Father Nature in a past life, because I am so drawn to looking at what's become of Mother Nature. So I stand at her deathbed, her hand in mine, and we wait.

"Live a little!"

"Happy New Year!"

I can't live a little, and I don't find anything happy about this new year.

Brian Trusiewicz
Sacred Heart High School, Waterbury, Connecticut

Quest for Truth

by Jodi Triplett

A lonely howl broke the silence, followed immediately by another, and yet another. Shivering, the old woman latched the door and the shutters against the noise. She sat down once more at her loom and began to weave. So intent on her work was she, that she didn't even hear someone entering.

"And what do you weave tonight?" asked a deep voice.

"The waves of the ocean have caught the moonbeams and taken them far away; I must get them back," answered the old woman.

"So you weave a net?" he asked.

"Come and see," she replied. The loom revealed a silken net, strung in the water which bobbed it gently up and down. Inside the net lay a gossamer butterfly, drinking nectar from a pale rose. "To lure the water, for it loves pretty things," she explained.

"In which case you had better watch out, or it will come for you!" laughed Eli. It is only a strange picture on a loom, he thought to himself, born of this old woman's mind.

"A loom on which I created the world and can

change it," she replied, unperturbed.

"Creator of the world!" scoffed Eli. As he went back along the forest trail, he muttered to himself, "Why, everyone knows she is just a crazy old woman who thinks she created the world." Comforted, he went on.

Another howl sounded, very close to where Eli was walking. Suddenly, a dozen gray shadows were about him. Flickering yellow eyes regarded him calmly.

"Hello," said Eli gravely.

A voice deep with age and wisdom replied, "Why did you go there?"

"I don't know why exactly," he said, "but she thinks she created the world."

A sound which was surprisingly like laughter passed through the pack of wolves. "Why," said the voice, "that is impossible since it was I and my pack who made the world."

"Then why did you make humans?" asked Eli, mystified.

"A mistake," was the sad reply. The wolves were gone as quickly as they had come, and Eli proceeded on.

A gentle river flowed quietly past him, visiting the sea. Eli asked the river if she had seen any moonbeams. "Here," the melodic, slurred voice of the river said. A patch of light made the river dance. "But the ocean has stolen all the rest away!" Eli did not know what to do, and began to walk on, but the river called him back.

"Wait!" she pleaded. "I know what you are thinking," she said. "I know I was foolish to create the ocean, who is selfish, but I know I made a mistake."

"Then why can't you simply take it away, if you created the world as you imply?" asked Eli.

"I cannot, for it is against life itself. But the flowing of my tears makes the ocean salty, so you know that I grieve for my mistakes."

Puzzled, Eli walked on and the river did not try to stop him. "Everyone says they created the world; I wonder who really did?" he mused.

"Why of course everyone knows *I* did," said a gravelly voice.

"Who said that?" demanded Eli.

"I did," replied the voice, directly underfoot. The path on which he was walking was the speaker. "I direct the lives of all my creations by making a place for them to see where they are going," continued the path.

"What happens if someone strays from the path?" questioned Eli.

"I am always here for them to come back to," was the reply.

"I don't believe you," Eli said. "Everyone keeps telling me this."

Angry, the path disappeared. Eli said he was sorry and asked if the path would please come back. The path came back immediately and led him on without comment down a dew-soaked hill. Grass grew lushly on either side of him and distant hills overhung the scene. A fine mist hung low over the hills, adding an ethereal quality.

"I can show you all the beauties of the world," the path said, and Eli agreed, looking about him.

A sudden image in Eli's mind of the silken net made him ask if the path knew of any moonbeams.

"The sea took them, stole them from me!" The path disappeared, and no coaxing on Eli's part could get it back.

Eli walked on, and soon his feet were soaked. The distant sound of water led him on, and soon salty spray clung delicately to his face. The slight mist turned into a heavy fog which obscured his vision. The sandy beach upon which he trod wound around the hills, patiently enduring the steady abuse of pounding ocean waves. A large wave broke spitefully over his knees and Eli angrily informed the ocean that everything he had heard about it was true. The ocean stilled suddenly, making everything quiet.

"And just what have you heard?" demanded its gruff voice.

"That you are selfish, and turned against your creators, going even so far as to steal the beautiful moonbeams," replied Eli.

"Humph. That's not true at all! The rivers all come to me—I don't force them here—and I always give some of myself to the clouds so the rivers may stay flowing. As for turning against my creators, how could I when I created everything?"

"Well—" began Eli.

"And moonbeams," the ocean swept on, ignoring his rather lame beginning. "The moonbeams play across me all the time; I have not stolen them. They come and go."

Suddenly, the ocean began to churn violently. Eli backed up, alarmed.

"No!" cried the ocean. "No, you cannot take them!"

Eli turned and saw the old woman. In her hands

lay a silken net, parted just enough to reveal a butterfly and a single rose.

"No," repeated the ocean in an anguished voice.
Unperturbed, the old woman cast her net and
waited. Huge waves broke over the beach in an effort to shake off the net, but the net bobbed indiffer-
ently in the water. The fog thinned as a faint outline
of the sun appeared in the distant hills. Moonbeams
fluttered gently across the ocean, ready to leave, and
then saw the net. The beams gently reached for the
butterfly and were caught. Pale morning light
streamed across the water and the moonbeams were
gone. The old woman calmly handed Eli the net and
told him to set them free far away from the ocean,
or it would take them again. She left, and Eli was
left alone except for the quiet weeping of the griev-
ing ocean.

Eli went on, but the crying of the ocean could be
heard long after he could no longer see it. The sun
was still low in the sky, laboring to bring warmth.
He paused against an outcropping of the rock to
rest.

"Why, I haven't seen the like of this in ages!" exclaimed a hoarse voice.

"Magic," agreed another.

"I'm sorry," the first voice said seeing Eli. "I am
Jorfin, creator of the world."

"And I am Filina, who has to put up with this tiring old fool."

Eli looked more closely and found that the two
who had spoken were the massive outcroppings of
rock upon which he sat, and a slender fir tree.

"Magic?" Eli began.

"Never mind now, go on and it will become clear in time." Eli resignedly walked on.

He was tired, and weeds held him back from his way. Eli suddenly remembered the path and called for it. "Of course I am here," the path spoke up, and Eli walked on contentedly. "As I was saying before, I will show you all the places of beauty."

That afternoon was one that Eli would not soon forget. The path led him through clear, meandering brooks and tall, ancient forests. Snowcapped mountains and lonely ridges were silhouetted in the distance. Ponds held plump frogs that sang of summer. Eagles screamed of the fierce joy of the kill, and foxes spoke of sly tricks and cleverness. Grass swayed gently under the silent shadows of the setting sun, and trees whispered of ancient, untold years. The wonder of the forest told a beautiful, yet forbidding story. "I can lead you nowhere else," said the path, and was gone.

Eli proceeded, alone but for the silken net which he clutched tightly to his chest, and came upon a small clearing. Leaning against a tree, he suddenly realized how tired he was. Remembering the moonbeams, he opened the net. In the gathering dusk, the moonbeams streaked beautifully into the sky.

Beneath the bright beams, Eli suddenly saw clearly. Far off, in the heavens, he could hear laughter as the creator of the world examined Eli's journey and found it humorous.

Jodi Triplett
Cheney Junior High School, Cheney, Washington

Goodbye, Grandpa

by Jeremy Zinn

Grandpa, look what I found!" And in the dust, between the railroad tracks, there was the stub of a flare.

"That's a flare," said Grandpa. "Train engineers use those to signal people when a train is coming."

Then there was a rumbling. We moved off the tracks and onto the grass. We both sat down in its coolness. We watched the small dot get bigger. The rumbling got louder and louder. Then the train was upon us. Grandpa and I recited the colors of the train as it went by. "Red, blue, yellow, green, white, red, blue, yellow, green, white." The train got faster and faster and we recited the colors faster and faster. When the last car was running by we said, "And there goes the good old caboose!" We laughed and laughed and laughed, even though we had done this every day for a long time.

Then there was a blur; my eyes popped open like a toaster. I whipped off the covers and started running downstairs. On the way down I ran into Mom. She said, "Whoa, whoa, where are you going so fast, Johnny?"

Making sure I wouldn't forget the dream, I blurted

out, "I'm going to tell Grandpa something."

In the distance my mother said "Johnny" in a worried voice. But my name was not fast enough to catch me today. I ran right into his room. My eyes were focused on the bed where he always lay, but "always" was not now. The white bed tortured me with no one in it.

"No, you can't leave me now. Please come back; you have been gone long enough. I miss you." My words were drowned out by sobs. "I miss you" echoed through the room.

"I miss Grandpa, too," said a voice. I looked, and there was Mom standing at the doorway. Then she continued, "You must remember he is not coming back, but he can still live in your mind."

"That's not good enough," I said as I stomped up to my room. I looked back, and there was Mom standing in the doorway, staring at the bed and probably thinking about dinner.

I went into my room and sat at my desk. I challenged myself to pick up everything from my floor and then pile it on my desk. Higher, higher, higher, lean, BOOM! I laughed. This was fun. I looked at my feet. There stood the elephant. It was a beautiful elephant carved from oak. Grandpa had given it to me. I remembered, as if it were yesterday.

"Good morning, Grandpa."

"Good morning, Johnny. Come here. I have something for you." I looked at the little animal.

"What is it?" I said.

"It's an elephant that I made when I was a little boy."

"What are those things sticking out of his face?"

"Those are tusks. They are made out of ivory."

"Oh! I know what that is. It's the stuff that tastes bad."

"When have you tasted ivory?"

"When I have been bad."

"Oh, that's Ivory Soap," said Grandpa. My face turned red.

"Time for dinner!" I blinked and awoke from my daydream. I had thought tusks were made out of Ivory Soap. But then I reassured myself by saying, "But that was when I was stupid; now I can add!"

Mom was a little sad during dinner but cheered up when she saw that I was in a better mood. After dinner I got into my pajamas and went to bed at the usual time. That night I lay in bed staring at the ceiling and listening to the hum of the fan. I thought to myself, 'Maybe if I think hard enough I can continue my dream.'

"Grandpa, what do you think it's like on the moon?" I said as he handed me my rod with a nice big worm on a hook.

"Well, I think it will look a little like Colorado, with mountains, cool streams, high meadows, and flowing waterfalls."

"I think gypsies live there, and they dance and sing all night and they explore all day. When are we going to the moon, Grandpa?"

"Let's see, we've made the hot air balloon, but we have to figure out how to blow the balloon up." Then he pulled in another big fish and slipped it onto the fish string.

"Grandpa, how are we going to eat all these fish?"

I said.

"Don't worry about that. Concentrate on getting that big fish you wanted." At that instant, there was a tug at the end of the line. "Do you need help?" said Grandpa.

"Nooo," I whined. "I'm almost six years old."

"That's pretty old," said Grandpa as he patted his warm hand on my back. "Pull it in. Pull it in," said Grandpa. With all my strength I pulled the fish in. The only people in the world were me, Grandpa, and the fish. Grandpa took the fish off the hook and let me touch it. That was the biggest fish I had ever caught. But then all happiness stopped.

I said, "Will the fish die?"

"Maybe."

"Will you die?"

Then Grandpa said, "This is something I want you to remember for your whole life: God is the fisherman who pulls us out of the sea and into the light." Then there was a blur.

In the silent and pitch-black night I said, "Goodnight, Grandpa."

Jeremy Zinn
Hawken School, Lyndhurst, Ohio

Story Index

Stories indexed for use as writing models

Character Development

Description and Setting

Dialogue

Personal Essay

Plot and Action

Reflection and Reminiscence

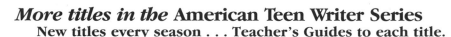